Apple Blossom Cologne Company Audit Case

Fifth Edition

Jack Paul
Lehigh University

McGraw-Hill Irwin

Boston Burr Ridge, IL Dubuque, IA Madison, WI New York San Francisco St. Louis
Bangkok Bogotá Caracas Kuala Lumpur Lisbon London Madrid Mexico City
Milan Montreal New Delhi Santiago Seoul Singapore Sydney Taipei Toronto

Publisher: *Brent Gordon*
Sponsoring editor: *Stewart Mattson*
Developmental editor: *Timothy Matray*
Marketing manager: *Rich Kolosa*
Production supervisor: *Michael McCormick*
Supplement producer: *Vicki Laird*
Cover Image: Adam Rooke

McGraw-Hill Higher Education

*A Division of The **McGraw-Hill** Companies*

Apple Blossom Cologne Company Audit Case
Jack Paul

Published by McGraw-Hill/Irwin, an imprint of the McGraw-Hill Companies, Inc., 1221 Avenue of the Americas, New York, NY 10020.

9 0 BKM/BKM 0 9 8

ISBN-13: 978-0-07-246644-7

ISBN-13: 0-07-246644-8

www.mhhe.com

Preface

To make the audit manageable, it is has been segmented into transaction cycles. For flexibility in assigning materials, exercises related to analysis of controls within the various cycles are optional. These exercises can be assigned as time permits. Consequently, the case is flexible enough to allow a more abbreviated "balance sheet" approach depending on classroom circumstances, the nature of the course, and the instructor's preferences.

Whether or not the optional exercises covering the detailed control analysis are assigned, the narratives and internal control questionnaires can be used to prepare flowcharts and assess control risk. After having performed the assessment of control risk, the student is in a position to write his or her audit program. The prior period working papers have been included to provide the student with a framework for (1) *designing the current year's audit program*, (2) *preparing the current year's working papers*, and (3) *assembling the completed case.* It should be noted that the prior year working paper file is purposefully left incomplete to preclude copying and to encourage originality.

New to this edition:

(1) An expanded explanation of how to proceed with the audit is included in the Introduction, as well as an index that cross-references the various exhibits to the case assignments.
(2) Assignment #1 has been expanded to include a broader analysis of risks in the planning stage of the audit.
(3) Risk model exercises have been removed from the assignments and included as an optional exercise in Assignment #4.
(4) Working papers based on the client's computer system have been included to improve on the realism of the case.
(5) Optional internal control exercises are based on the client's computer-based LAN system.
(6) A disk included with the Instructor's Manual contains general audit programs that can, at the instructor's discretion, be used as a starting point for tailoring audit programs for the client's situation.

I would like to express my appreciation to Vivian Kroner, CPA, CMA, who reviewed the entire manuscript, for her helpful suggestions and comments.

Jack W. Paul

Table of Contents

I
General Instructions and Preparations

Apple Blossom Cologne Company
Audit Case

The Apple Blossom Cologne Company audit case illustrates the application of basic auditing principles in a small company audit situation. This case is designed for familiarization with fundamental audit principles, procedures, and working papers . . . *it by no means exhausts the complexities of a thorough and complete audit*! Because of this design limitation, the case does not include all auditing procedures required in an actual audit.

Problem assignments include the following:
(1) internal control questionnaire
(2) instructions and explanations
(3) evidence to be used during your audit
(4) client-prepared schedules
(5) forms for flowcharting the accounting cycle, analyzing control procedures, and assessing control risk (Assignments 2, 3, 4, 8, and 9–optional); in Assignment #4, you also calculate detection risk
(6) a form for the audit program listing some of the assertions you will be testing in your work.

In all assignments, you will be required to obtain an understanding of internal control and prepare a substantive audit program for balances and/or transactions. The auditor first considers the financial statement assertions and then devises audit objectives. The financial statement assertions serve as a focal point around which procedures may be grouped to form an audit program. The financial statement assertions are:[1]

(1) **Existence or Occurrence**–the client asserts that assets and liabilities actually exist and that sales and expense transactions actually occurred.

(2) **Completeness**–the client asserts that all transactions and accounts which should be presented in the financial statements are included.

(3) **Rights and Obligations**–the client asserts that the company has rights to the assets and that liabilities are the obligations of the company at a given date.

(4) **Valuation or Allocation**–the client asserts that asset, liability, revenue, and expense items have been included in the financial statements at appropriate amounts.

(5) **Presentation and Disclosure**–the client asserts that financial statement components are properly classified, described, and disclosed.

Once you have considered the financial statement assertions, you can more easily derive audit objectives pertaining to each area. For example, as to the assertion whether accounts receivable exist, the auditor's objective is to obtain and evaluate evidence concerning this assertion. To achieve this objective, the auditor might send letters of confirmation to determine whether receivables do in fact exist.

---

[1]AICPA Professional Standards, Volume 1 (New York: American Institute of Certified Public Accountants, 2000), AU Sec. 326.03-.08. Copyright 2000 American Institute of Certified Public Accountants, Inc.

ASSESSING AUDIT RISK

Audit risk (AR) is the probability that the auditor unknowingly fails to modify the opinion regarding an assertion that is materially in error (for example, the assertion regarding the existence of accounts receivable). Audit risk is composed of three separate risks. These risks may be defined as follows:[2]

- **Inherent Risk (IR)** - the susceptibility of an assertion to a material misstatement, assuming there are no related internal control structure policies or procedures. Inherent risk can be viewed as the probability that material errors occur in the process leading to the preparation of the financial statements.

- **Control Risk (CR)** - the risk that a material misstatement that could occur in an assertion will not be prevented or detected on a timely basis by an entity's internal control structure policies or procedures. Control risk can be viewed as the probability that, given errors have occurred, internal control does not prevent, detect, or correct these errors.

- **Detection risk (DR)** - the risk that the auditor will not detect a material misstatement that exists in an assertion. Detection risk can be viewed as the probability that the auditor does not detect material errors in the financial statements, given that such errors occur and internal control fails to detect them.

These components can be combined to formulate the *audit risk model*:

$$AR = IR \times CR \times DR.$$

This model is a tool that provides the auditor with a starting point for determining the nature (type), extent (quantity), and timing of the audit tests. Audit risk should be set at a relatively low level. Inherent risk is not controllable by the auditor; it must be estimated. Control risk, also not controllable by the auditor, is assessed after analyzing internal control. The auditor can control detection risk by modifying the nature, extent, and timing of evidence. By increasing the effectiveness of evidence through changing the *type* of evidence, by obtaining *more* evidence, or by shifting the *timing* of the audit tests closer to the balance sheet date, the auditor can reduce detection risk to an acceptable level.

For example, assume the auditor is working on accounts receivable. The auditor would like to assure that the risk of material nonexistent accounts does not exceed .05. Accordingly, the desired assurance (confidence) that there are no material fictitious accounts is 95% (1 - .05). Assume that the auditor has assessed inherent risk at .60. This assessment means that the auditor is 40% confident (1 - .60) that material fictitious accounts have not found their way into the client's receivables. We can state that the auditor has 40% confidence in the nature of the account. The auditor has assessed control risk at .30. This assessment means that the auditor is 70% (1 - .30) confident that internal control would detect and correct material misstatements of accounts receivable due to nonexistent accounts. On the basis of these inherent and control risk assessments, the detection risk acceptable to the auditor is found to be .28, calculated as follows:

$$DR = \frac{AR}{IR \times CR} = \frac{.05}{.60 \times .30} = .28.$$

---

[2] See AICPA Professional Standards, Volume 1 (New York: American Institute of Certified Public Accountants, 2000) AU Sec 319A.67. Copyright 2000 American Institute of Certified Public Accountants, Inc.

What does a detection risk of .28 imply? This is the detection risk acceptable to the auditor. The auditor has to examine sufficient substantive evidence to reduce the risk of not detecting a fictitious account to .28. Consequently, the auditor has to have 72% (1 - .28) confidence in this substantive evidence after the testing has been completed. When this confidence is combined with the confidence obtained from the assessments of the nature of the account (40%) and internal control (70%), the overall audit confidence will be 95%. This is the confidence level obtained from *all* the evidence regarding the presence of material fictitious accounts receivable. The overall audit risk (AR) for this assertion is therefore .05.

What would constitute sufficient substantive evidence? With regard to the *nature* of the evidence, the auditor may decide to send confirmation letters. Regarding *extent*, the auditor may elect to confirm only the largest accounts. With respect to *timing*, the auditor may determine that it is not necessary to confirm the receivables at the end of the year. If the acceptable detection risk were *lower* than .28, the auditor would have to obtain *more* evidence to provide more confidence. If the acceptable detection risk were *higher* than .28, the auditor could collect *less* evidence since less confidence would be needed in the substantive testing.

For a variety of reasons, it is not feasible in a case like this to determine the nature, extent, and timing of substantive testing on the basis of inherent and control risk assessments. Nevertheless, the audit risk model can provide an *indication* of the degree to which evidence has to be gathered in a specific instance. The model is a convenient *planning tool* and a good *starting point* for specifying substantive testing. Exercises in this case related to the calculation of detection risk are found in Assignment 4, Inventory and Purchases. These tasks are *optional.* Your instructor will tell you if you are to work these exercises.

CONTROL RISK ASSESSMENT

Assignments 1, 3, 4, 8 and 9 specifically deal with a cycle and contain optional exercises requiring that you flowchart the system, formally analyze internal control strengths and weaknesses, and assess control risk. These optional exercises precede the required substantive exercises in these assignments.

Flowcharting

You should use flowcharting software if you are directed by your instructor to flowchart systems. The following assignments include flowcharting:

Assignment	Topic
#1	Integration of Accounting System
#2	Revenues and Accounts Receivable Processing
#3	Cash Receipts and Cash Disbursements Processing
#4	Inventory-Purchases Processing
#8	Accounts Payable Processing
#9	Payroll Processing

Use the following flowchart symbols when preparing your flowcharts:

Document - Input document or output report.

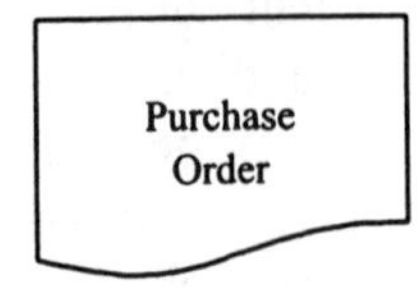

Journal or Ledger - Designates a journal or ledger.

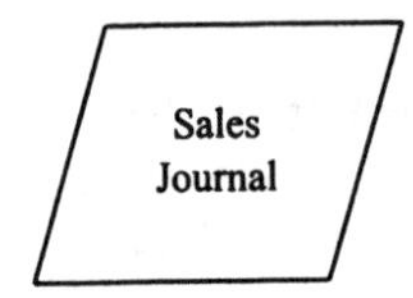

Terminal - To show the beginning or ending of the flowchart or the receipt or transmittal of information.

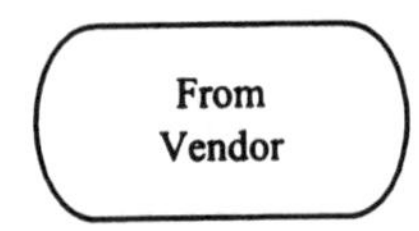

Decision - Symbol to indicate that a particular action is required.

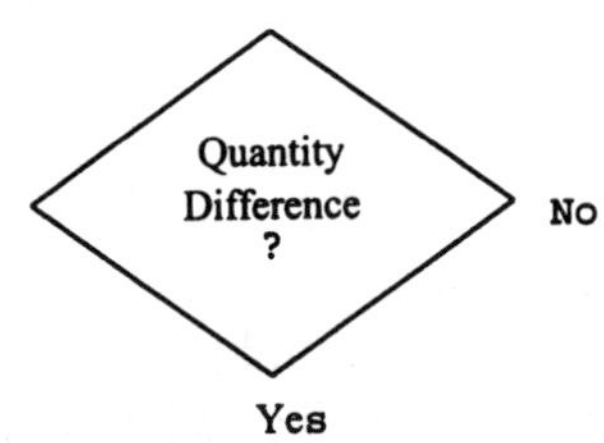

Filing Symbol - To show by whom and in what particular manner documents are filed.

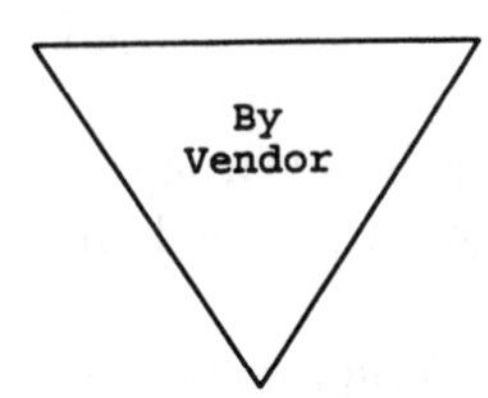

Annotation – Used to explain what actions are taking place at various points in the system.

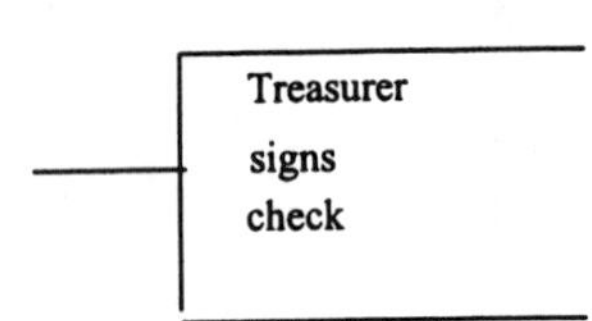

Flowlines - Used to show the flow of data within the system.

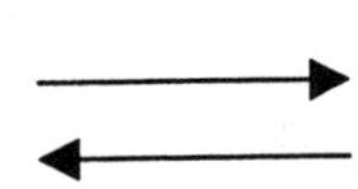

Keying – Indicates input by typing or keying in data.

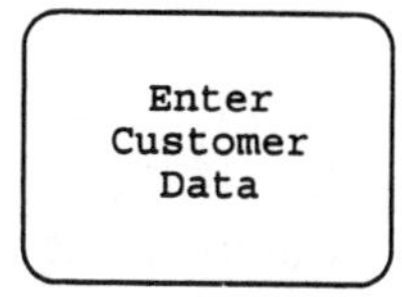

Process – Used to designate a software process.

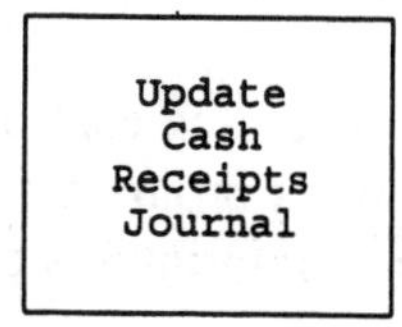

File – Symbol indicating a file stored on a diskette or hard drive.

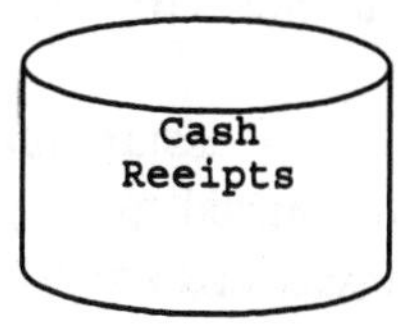

The Control Environment

The control environment provides the auditor with an indication of the effectiveness of the accounting system and control activities. The control environment comprises the following factors:

1. Integrity and ethical values
2. The company's commitment to competence
3. The participation of the board of directors or audit committee
4. Management's philosophy and operating style
5. Organizational structure
6. Assignment of authority and responsibility
7. Human resource policies and practices.

The auditor examines each of these factors to assess their impact on control activities and the accounting system.

Control Activities

The optional control structure exercises in Assignments 2, 3, 4, 8 and 9 direct you to list control activities and to provide possible tests of those controls. Tests of controls are used to determine whether control policies and procedures are functioning as the auditor has been led to believe from the systems narratives and the internal control questionnaire. As you go through the systems narratives (found in the Permanent File materials) and the internal control questionnaires, you should keep in mind six categories of control activities. Use these control categories as a basis for analyzing control strengths and weaknesses and for determining the possible errors and/or irregularities that could occur in each system.

The six categories of control activities consist of two *general control* categories and four *specific control* categories. The general controls provide reasonable assurance that the accounting control system is functioning properly. The four specific control categories are applicable to the processing of transactions.

General Controls. Controls that provide reasonable assurance the specific controls are functioning properly:

- **Segregation of functions**–Minimizes incompatible functions.

- **Access to Assets**–Provides proper safeguarding of assets and records by restricting access only to authorized personnel.

In addition to the preceding controls, general controls in an information technology (IT) environment include such considerations as program controls, passwords and data encryption for restricting access to programs and data, logs for monitoring system usage, and so on.

Specific (or Application) Controls. These controls monitor the processing of transactions. Specific controls *follow the flow of transactions* from initiation of the transaction to follow-up. In an IT environment, these types of controls are normally referred to as *application controls*:

- **Authorization**–To assure that transactions are executed in accordance with the specific or general authorization required to engage the company in transactions of the particular type and to ensure that only valid transactions are processed.

- **Input controls**–To assure that all transactions that should be recorded in the accounts are recorded in the correct amounts and are posted to the appropriate accounts. Implies both completeness (the capturing of all transactions) and accuracy of data entry (in correct amount and to correct account). Includes numerical sequencing and control of documents, control totals, input edit checks, key verification, check digits, logic tests, holding files, and so on.

- **Processing controls**–To assure that computations affecting the accounts are correctly performed. Includes, for example, clerical checks, programmed edit tests, logical tests, validity tests, completeness tests, and document matching.

- **Output controls**–Designed to assure that the output data are correct. Output controls include reconciliations, user reviews of output and exception reports, and comparison of assets with recorded accountability by means of physical counts.

Tests of Controls

The following tests of controls are typical of those used by the auditor to test control activities:

(1) **Observation**–includes observation of control functions and an awareness of events; examples are observation of the safeguarding of assets and the segregation of duties.

(2) **Verbal inquiry**–this procedure involves the collection of oral evidence, for example from management or employees to determine the reasonableness of recorded purchase transactions.

(3) **Vouching**–examination of documents. Following an item backward from a financial record to a supporting document; used, for example, to find approvals on documents or signatures on checks.

(4) **Sequence checking**–involves examining serially numbered documents to assure that no documents are missing.

(5) **Direct examination**–includes, for example, the examination of (1) bank reconciliations, (2) sales invoices to determine whether supporting shipping documents are present, (3) minutes for approvals, and (4) the chart of accounts for accuracy.

(6) **Tracing**–the opposite of vouching. Tracing forward through the accounting system from source documents to records, for example to determine whether postings were made.

In the optional control structure exercises found in Assignments 2, 3, 4, 8 and 9, you will also be asked to list weaknesses and possible errors or irregularities, as well as compensating substantive procedures. After you have examined the control strengths and weaknesses, you will be in a position to assess control risk and then prepare your substantive audit program.

SUBSTANTIVE TESTING

Audit Programs

One of the more important aspects of your auditing course is learning the procedures required for the various audit areas. With this in mind, the starting point for each assignment, other than the optional internal control exercises in Assignments 2, 3, 4, 8 and 9, is the preparation of a substantive audit program for the particular account or group of accounts. You are expected to determine the necessary audit steps from the prior period working papers, the Permanent File material, internal control questionnaire, problem narrative, the working papers and evidence provided with each problem assignment, and from your textbook. In a real audit situation, the in-charge auditor in the field is responsible for writing an audit program to fit the current year audit engagement. *Placing this responsibility on you in this audit case will increase your ability to assume that decision-making responsibility.*

If control risk can be assessed at less than the maximum level of 100%, the auditor can restrict substantive tests needed to gather sufficient competent evidence as required by the third standard of field work. To assess control risk, the auditor obtains an understanding of internal control and determines the potential errors or irregularities that may occur in order to develop the substantive audit program. An auditor first considers the financial statement assertions and devises audit objectives. Next, the auditor should specify control objectives and relate these control objectives to the financial statement assertions, since the control objectives established by management, if achieved, should help the auditor fulfill the audit objectives. The assertions may be related to general control objectives as follows:

Management Assertion	*Related General Control Objective*
Existence or occurrence	Validity
Completeness	Completeness
Rights and obligations	Authorization
Valuation or allocation	Valuation
Presentation and disclosure	Classification

Next the auditor would enumerate specific control objectives for the particular account or class of transactions being audited. Then the auditor enumerates the control activities (the strengths) of the system under review, relates them to the internal control objectives and determines whether the controls actually achieve the control objectives by performing tests of controls. The auditor also considers the weaknesses and the possible substantive errors that may occur because of those weaknesses. By keeping the potential errors in mind, as well as the strengths in the system, you will be in a position to prepare your substantive audit program.

In writing a substantive audit program for balances and/or transactions, it is important to recognize management's financial statement assertions, the auditor's audit objectives, and the impact of internal control required to formulate a testable hypothesis. A problem hypothesis is formulated in the manner of a financial statement assertion; for example: "The recorded accounts receivable exist." The auditor begins to write the audit program by explicitly recognizing management's assertions regarding the propriety of the accounting records and amounts. He or she then lists evidence-gathering procedures which, when performed, would either support or refute the assertions. Throughout this audit case, whenever you are asked to write a substantive audit program, a few of the assertions typical of that assignment are listed for you. Add other assertions you think are appropriate and then write your program to collect the required evidence.

Substantive Tests

Substantive procedures consist of tests of details of transactions and balances, as well as analytical procedures. Common substantive tests include.:

(1) **Recalculation**–the auditor checks calculations performed by client personnel. This is a type of mathematical evidence.

(2) **Physical observation**–this procedure includes the observation of tangible assets and formal documents such as securities and mortgages.

(3) **Confirmation**–direct correspondence with independent parties.

(4) **Verbal inquiry**–this procedure involves the collection of oral evidence from independent parties and client officials.

(5) **Vouching**–examination of documents. Vouching entails following an item from an account backwards through the accounting system to find the source documentation that supports the item selected.

(6) **Tracing**–the opposite of vouching. The auditor selects a sample source document and traces forward through the accounting system to verify that the final recording of the item is correct.

(7) **Scanning**–review documentation looking for anything unusual in order to identify such items for vouching or tracing.

(8) **Analytical procedures**–the computation and study of financial ratios and amounts. Includes (a) ratio and trend analysis, (b) comparisons with prior years, (c) reference to statistical data produced by independent agencies, and (d) analysis of interrelationships with other data, including related accounts.

PREPARATIONS BEFORE BEGINNING THE ASSIGNMENTS

The administrative office and plant facility of Apple Blossom Cologne Company are located at 1308 Bee Hive Boulevard in Chicago, Illinois. The company is a wholesale distributor of fruit-scented cremes, lotions, oils, colognes, and spray perfumes. More information about the company history and organization is included in the Permanent File materials presented later.

Your auditing firm of Anderson, Olds, and Watershed has performed an annual audit of Apple Blossom Cologne Company since 1989. For the past several years Jasper Parsons, a senior with your firm, performed the audit. Jasper Parsons has left the firm, and you have been assigned as senior auditor in charge of the Apple Blossom Cologne Company audit for the year ended December 31, 2003.

Jasper Parsons completed the interim work. He also completed the internal control questionnaires with the Controller, Parker Shelton, on December 15, 2003 and updated the internal control narratives at that time. You are to perform your examination in accordance with generally accepted auditing standards and make such tests of the accounting records and perform such other auditing procedures as you consider necessary in the circumstances.

Apple Blossom is a small company and you will be performing all of the audit procedures yourself except where the instructions indicate that an assistant has helped you by performing the audit work on selected accounts. You may assume that the following tasks have been performed in preparation for this audit:

(1) On December 15, 2003, Jasper Parsons completed the internal control questionnaire.

(2) On December 29, 2003, you reviewed prior year's working papers and financial statements of Apple Blossom Cologne Company.

(3) On December 30, 2003, you visited the client's plant and were introduced to the client's personnel. You arranged to have various working paper schedules prepared for you by Don McKenna, an accountant in the controller's office.

(4) On Wednesday, December 31, 2003, you obtained control of, counted, and returned to the client the undeposited cash receipts and the petty cash fund. You also examined securities on this date.

(4) On Thursday, January 1, 2004, you observed client personnel taking the physical inventory, recorded test counts, and wrote an inventory observation memorandum.

(5) On Friday, January 2, 2004, with the client's assistance, you prepared and mailed all necessary correspondence dealing with confirmations of receivable balances, confirmations of bank balances, cutoff bank statements, accounts and notes payable confirmations, and attorney's letter.

You plan to begin your audit on Monday, January 12, 2004, with an expected completion date of Friday, February 6, 2004. You have received a number of replies from the confirmations, and others will come in as your work proceeds. You have in your possession the various working papers and schedules that Don McKenna prepared for you. In addition, the client's books have been closed for the year, and working trial balances of the balance sheet and income statement accounts have been prepared. From your office you will bring last year's audit working papers and the Permanent File on the Apple Blossom Cologne Company.

The current year's trial balances are included in Section IV, which follows immediately after Assignment # 12. As you proceed with the audit work, you will find items for which adjusting or correcting entries may be required. ***The president of Apple Blossom has stated that he wishes to adjust the company's records for every such item you discover.*** **Maintain a list of these adjusting entries and post them to working paper AJE (Proposed Adjusting Journal Entries working paper) included in Section IV (see working paper AJE in the prior year's working papers for an example of the proper format). Since each adjustment that you find will be "booked" by the client, post each entry to the trial balance, to the working paper giving rise to the adjustment, and to working paper AJE. Prepare these adjustments as you proceed with the audit.**

As an auditor you are required to communicate to the Board of Directors matters concerning the internal control structure that may be of interest to the Board. These matters are termed "reportable conditions." A reportable condition is a matter representing a significant deficiency in the design or operation of the internal control structure that may preclude the preparation of accurate financial data. Cognizant of this, you should perform your audit work with the intent of identifying for possible management action, those areas of internal control that you consider deficient. When completing the audit (see Assignment 12), preparation of a letter pointing out the weaknesses or deficiencies found and suggesting possible corrective actions is included as an optional exercise.

You may assume that you have read all minutes of stockholder meetings and meetings of the Board of Directors. You have made notes of relevant items from the minutes and these are included in the Permanent File information. You should cross-reference items of accounting significance that you find in the minutes to appropriate working papers as you prepare them. You should review the Permanent File material (included immediately after these general instructions) before beginning your audit work.

Calendars for two months surrounding the balance sheet date are as follows:

December 2003

SU	MO	TU	WE	TH	FR	SA
	1	2	3	4	5	6
7	8	9	10	11	12	13
14	15	16	17	18	19	20
21	22	23	24	25	26	27
28	29	30	31			

January 2004

SU	MO	TU	WE	TH	FR	SA
				1	2	3
4	5	6	7	8	9	10
11	12	13	14	15	16	17
18	19	20	21	22	23	24
25	26	27	28	29	30	31

PRIOR YEAR'S WORKING PAPERS

The prior year's working papers are an important resource for completing the current year's audit. The prior year's working papers section is the place to start your work, and you should refer to these working papers often. The prior year's working papers should be used as a starting point for preparing the audit program. They should also be used as a guide for preparing the current year's audit working papers. Please note that the prior year's file includes the basic working papers you will need to complete the audit but does not include all items that would be found in an actual audit situation. You should refer to your textbook to obtain examples of a complete working paper file. Other sources are also available. For example, public accounting firms publish information on working paper files and often make this information available to colleges and universities. Information is also available through the American Institute of Certified Public Accountants (www.aicpa.org).

Turn to the prior year's working papers in Section V. Notice the way the section is laid out, beginning with aggregated information (senior's summary, audit opinion, financial statements, and summary of internal control) and moving to the support of this summarized information on the detailed working papers.

Examine the trial balance (TB-BS and TB-IS) prepared by the senior. Notice the form of cross referencing from the supporting working papers. Each significant number on the trial balance is supported by a working paper that documents the accumulation of audit evidence. For example, the accounts payable balances–per books and per audit–on the trial balance are supported by working paper G-1. Turn to this working paper. Notice the tick marks following the suppliers' account balances listed on G-1. These tick marks refer to audit evidence verifying the accuracy of the balance. In addition, notice the cross references to working papers G-3 and G-4. Working papers G-3 and G-4 are confirmations of balances with suppliers. Also notice that working paper G-1 is affected by an audit adjustment that originates on working paper G-2. Examine the cross referencing to the trial balance and the way the adjustment has been set out on working paper G-1.

CURRENT YEAR S WORKING PAPER FILE

When you begin the audit, set up your current year's working paper file by assembling your working papers in a loose leaf binder. Use the style of working paper cross referencing found in the prior year's working paper file. **In general, each number on a working paper should be supported by a tick mark showing the evidence that corroborates that number, or to another working paper where the evidence can be found. You should place each audit adjustment you find on: (1) the working paper giving rise to the adjustment, (2) working paper AJE , and (3) the working trial balance.**

The audit program is an important part of the audit as it sets out the audit testing to be accomplished. Be very careful when preparing your programs to set out the specific steps in an understandable fashion. It is helpful to prepare your programs using word processing software. As you go through the audit, cross reference each program step that addresses a weakness in internal control to the appropriate question on the internal control questionnaire (e.g., Q-1, Q-2, etc.).

Assemble your current working papers in the following order:

(1) Senior's Audit Memorandum (from Assignment #12, an optional exercise)
(2) Planning working papers (from Assignment #1)
(3) Draft of audit report (from Assignment #12, an optional exercise)
(4) Draft of financial statements and footnotes (from Assignment #12, an optional exercise)
(5) Letter concerning deficiencies in internal control (from Assignment #12, an optional exercise)
(6) Working trial balances–balance sheet and income statement
(7) Schedule of adjusting journal entries
(8) Assignment working papers in working paper order (A, B, C, etc.); include internal control analyses (if applicable), and audit program(s) for each assignment with that assignment's working papers. (Alternatively, your instructor may wish you to place the internal control analyses, flowcharts, and so on, with the planning working papers)

WORKING PAPERS ON DISKETTE

If you wish to prepare the working papers using spreadsheet software–or if your instructor has directed you to do so-templates for the working papers in each assignment are included on the *ABC Working Papers* diskette. The files are in Excel format (.XLS).

In addition to the working papers found in the casebook, the time budget worksheet from Assignment #1, and the auditor's trial balances found in Section IV are on the diskette. Use the trial balance file for (1) performing analytical procedures, (2) preparing the financial statements, and (3) performing other computer-based applications as directed by your instructor.

List of Working Papers on the ABC Working Papers Diskette

A-1	Big City National Bank Reconciliation
A-3	Second National Bank Reconciliation
A-6	Undeposited Cash Receipts
A-7	Petty Cash
B-1	Accounts Receivable Aged Trial Balance
C-1	Inventory
C-2	Inventory Observation
E-2	Securities Examination
F-2	Additions to Property, Plant, and Equipment
F-3	Retirements of Property, Plant, and Equipment
F-4	Depreciation Computation
F-5	Repairs and Maintenance
G-1	Accounts Payable
H-1	Accrued Payroll Taxes
H-4	Federal Income Taxes Payable
P-1	Time Budget
TBBS-TBIS	Working Trial Balance

LIST OF EXHIBITS

The following exhibits are found in the various assignments. These exhibits contain information pertaining to documents and records of the client. *These documents and records belong to the client and are retained by the client.* The auditor uses them as evidence to support the audit opinion. Refer to this listing to determine which exhibits pertain to the different assignments.

	Contents of Exhibit	Assignment
Exhibit 1	Big City National Bank Cutoff Bank Statement	#3 Cash
Exhibit 2	Second National Bank Cutoff Bank Statement	#3 Cash
Exhibit 3	Cash Receipts Journal - December and January (selected portions)	#3 Cash
Exhibit 4	Cash Disbursements Journal - December and January (selected portions)	#3 Cash
Exhibit 5	Cash Vouchers for Inventory Purchases	#4 Inventory and Purchases
Exhibit 6	Cash Vouchers for Property, Plant, and Equipment	#7 Property, Plant, and Equipment

	Contents of Exhibit	Assignment
Exhibit 7	Cash Vouchers for Accounts Payable	#8 Accounts Payable Processing
Exhibit 8	Receiving Log - December and January Voucher Register - January	#8 Accounts Payable Processing

II
Permanent File Materials

Apple Blossom Cologne Company
History and Background

The Apple Blossom Cologne Company was founded as a wholesale distributor of scented perfumes in Chicago, Illinois on April 23, 1984. Today, the company handles an expanded line of fruit-scented cremes, lotions, oils, colognes, and spray perfumes. The company purchases large quantities of its products direct from various factory locations. The product is repackaged and distributed to retailers throughout the Chicago metropolitan area and a four-state area extending about 300 miles radially from the plant location.

The company was initially organized in Chicago as a partnership by James Martin and Larry Lancaster. James Martin had been the production manager of a well-known cosmetics manufacturer while Larry Lancaster was a salesman for the same company. Having noticed the role that a wholesaler could play in servicing smaller stores that could not obtain reasonable volume discounts from the larger manufacturers, they started the partnership in 1984, each contributing an equal amount of assets and receiving an equal share of the equity and income distribution. In order to obtain sufficient financing to expand the plant and operations, Martin and Lancaster agreed to incorporate the business in 1991.

The corporation was authorized to issue 20,000 shares of $100 par value common stock. Of the shares authorized, 6,000 were issued; 2,000 each to Martin and Lancaster and 1,000 each to Arthur Broman and Melissa Winchester. Martin and Lancaster took their shares in exchange for their interests in the partnership. Broman and Winchester paid cash for their shares. The capital provided by the sale of stock to Broman and Winchester allowed the company to expand its product lines. This expansion increased sales volume and profitability considerably.

The next stock distribution came in 1995 when 3,250 additional shares were issued. James Martin purchased 2,000 shares of the new issue for cash and the other 1,250 shares were issued for cash in small amounts to ten individuals not previously affiliated with the company. The company's stock is occasionally traded in the over-the-counter market.

In 1989, the Martin and Lancaster partnership needed to borrow money for working capital. The bank where they applied for the loan required a set of audited financial statements. The CPA firm of Anderson, Olds, and Watershed was engaged by Martin and Lancaster to perform the necessary audit. The audit of Apple Blossom Cologne Company has been a continuing engagement for Anderson, Olds, and Watershed since 1989 and the firm has given an unqualified opinion in each of those years. They also helped with the incorporation procedures in 1991.

Apple Blossom Cologne Company
Organizational Structure

The plant facility is comprised of six major areas: (1) receiving dock, (2) warehouse, (3) repackaging area, (4) shipping dock, (5) garage, and (6) office. A short description of each work area is as follows:

(1) **Receiving dock**–Goods are received directly from the suppliers' factories packaged in cases of 24 units each. Other supply items such as small tools, office supplies, repair parts, and small fixed assets are also received at the receiving dock. A receiving report and receiving log entry are prepared for all materials crossing this dock area.

(2) **Warehouse**–All inventory is held here for repackaging and shipment on customer order. All inventory is stored as received from the factory until a customer order is received.

(3) **Repackaging area**–On customer order, personnel in this area package the shipment according to customer specifications. Sometimes, units (bottles, cans, etc.) can be simply relabeled and shipped as received from the factory. Other orders call for more complex packaging like changing containers and re-labeling.

(4) **Shipping dock**–All materials leaving the plant facility cross this dock and a shipping report is prepared. Inventory shipments to customers comprise nearly all of total shipments.

(5) **Garage**–The company maintains a fleet of automobiles for their salespeople. These cars are serviced from this garage. Forklift tractors used in the repackaging area and delivery vehicles are also serviced and repaired here in the garage.

(6) **Office**–All offices in Apple Blossom Cologne Company are centralized.

Larry Lancaster has overall responsibility for the operation of the company. Louise McWhorter is the president's secretary. Theodore Brown, the production superintendent, has authority over operations of the plant, assisted by the production foreman, Terry Freitag. Under the foreman are three area supervisors; each supervisor employs several hourly paid production employees. There are fourteen such hourly production employees in all.

Ellen Jacobs is the sales manager; she has a staff of six salaried salespersons. Company salespersons call on Chicago customers at least once a week and out-of-town customers at least once a month. In addition, the office frequently receives calls directly from customers ordering products. Out-of-town customers are supplied with a catalog and frequently call in their orders. The credit manager, Brenda Robertson, coordinates her work between the sales area and the accounting department but reports to Ellen Jacobs. Simon Swift, the accounts receivable clerk, maintains the accounts receivable ledgers and assists Brenda Robertson.

In accounting, the controller, Parker Shelton has a bookkeeper (Donald McKenna) and an accounts payable clerk (Dave Dull) to assist him. The treasurer's duties are handled by Lillian Stockton assisted by a cashier, Pam Lewis.

The company is organized into five departments (1) administrative, (2) accounting, (3) financial, (4) production, and (5) sales. Information concerning the administrative, accounting, and related financial responsibilities of the various employees of Apple Blossom Cologne Company are as follows:

Each employee's departmental affiliation is designated by the following letter code:

A–Administrative Department
C–Accounting Department
F–Finance Department
P–Production Department
S–Sales Department.

Apple Blossom Cologne Company
Administrative, Accounting, and
Related Financial Responsibilities

President–Larry Lancaster (A)
1. Reports to Board of Directors
2. Overall authorization

Production Superintendent–Theodore Brown (P)
1. Reports to Larry Lancaster
2. Overall operation of plant

Sales Manager–Ellen Jacobs (S)
1. Reports to Larry Lancaster
2. Overall sales operations
3. Approves all sales orders
4. Supervises six salaried salespersons who prepare sales orders

Controller–Parker Shelton (C)
1. Reports to Larry Lancaster
2. Overall information processing (accounting)
3. Reconciles prelist
4. Signs checks (with treasurer, dual signature)
5. Approves journal entries

Treasurer–Lillian Stockton (F)
1. Reports to Larry Lancaster
2. Overall financial responsibility
3. Controls cash and investments
4. Signs checks (with controller, dual signature)
5. Makes daily bank deposit
6. Reconciles bank account

Secretary to President–Louise McWhorter (A)
1. Reports to Larry Lancaster
2. Corporate secretary
3. Maintains stock certificate book
4. Maintains personnel records and time cards

Bookkeeper–Donald McKenna (C)
1. Reports to Parker Shelton
2. Prepares journal entries and maintains general journal
3. Prepares various other detailed schedules as required
4. Maintains sales register and bills customers
5. Maintains payroll register
6. Maintains general ledger and prepares financial statements

Cashier–Pam Lewis (F)
1. Reports to Lillian Stockton
2. Maintains cash receipts journal
3. Prepares checks for signature
4. Prepares cash deposit

Credit Manager–Brenda Robertson (S)
1. Reports to Ellen Jacobs
2. Approves credit
3. Approves write-offs of delinquent accounts
4. Issues credit memos

Production Foreman–Terry Freitag (P)
1. Reports to Theodore Brown
2. Oversees production
3. Approves purchase orders

Inventory (Storeroom) Clerk–Anita Columbo (P)
1. Reports to Terry Freitag
2. Maintains perpetual inventory records
3. Issues and controls stock at the warehouse

Accounts Receivable Clerk–Simon Swift (S)
1. Reports to Brenda Robertson
2. Maintains accounts receivable subsidiary ledger
3. Prepares cash prelist

Accounts Payable Clerk–Dave Dull (C)
1. Reports to Parker Shelton
2. Maintains accounts payable subsidiary ledger
3. Maintains voucher register (purchases journal)
4. Maintains fixed asset subsidiary ledger
5. Distributes payroll checks
6. Mails checks to vendors

Mailroom Clerk–Gerald Klett (A)
1. Reports to Louise McWhorter
2. Opens mail

urchasing Agent–Cheryl Palmer (P)

. Reports to Theodore Brown
. Makes purchases
. Prepares purchase orders
. Maintains vendor invoice and receiving report file
. Maintains cash disbursements journal

eceiving Dock Manager–William Beauchamp (P)

. Reports to Terry Freitag
. Supervises receipt of merchandise
. Supervises two hourly employees

epackaging Area Manager–Marsha Doyle (P)

Reports to Terry Freitag
Overall order preparation
Supervises ten hourly employees

ipping Dock Manager–George Evershock (P)

Reports to Terry Freitag
Supervises shipping of merchandise
Supervises two hourly employees

Apple Blossom Cologne Company
Internal Control

Internal control consists of five components: control environment, risk assessment, control activities, the information (accounting) system, and monitoring control performance. Information regarding each of these components is provided in this section.

Control Environment

The control environment at Apple Blossom Cologne Company is considered to be good for a small company. Management fosters an atmosphere that enhances the effectiveness of control policies and procedures. Following are comments regarding each of the control environment factors:

(1) **Integrity and Ethical Values**–Our firm has been auditing Apple Blossom Cologne Company for over fourteen years. During that time, we have observed only the highest standards of integrity and ethical values among the officers and personnel at Apple Blossom.

(2) **Commitment to Competence**–Management is aware of the need to place competent people. The various departments carry out training. For the most part, the personnel at Apple Blossom are well trained and competent.

(3) **Board of Directors or Audit Committee Participation**–Apple Blossom is a small company. As such, management does not believe that a formal audit committee is necessary. The controller and the treasurer continually monitor the financial progress of the company. In addition, Larry Lancaster and James Martin act as liaison with our firm.

(4) **Management's Philosophy and Operating Style**–Management believes that controls are important. Department heads periodically meet with employees to discuss financial and managerial policies and procedures, including adequate controls.

(5) **Organizational Structure**–Management has not prepared a formal organization chart. Because of the small size of the company, each individual knows his or her duties and responsibilities.

(6) **Assignment of Authority and Responsibility**–Job descriptions are maintained by the personnel manager in a personnel policy manual. In addition, because of the size of the company, each individual is aware of his or her assigned duties. No formal ethical code of conduct has been prepared, but our firm has had no reason to doubt the honesty of management or other employees.

(7) **Human Resource Policies and Practices**–There are no formal training or promotion policies. Hiring, promotion, and dismissal are carried out by the various department heads after consultation with Mr. Lancaster. The Board sets compensation for all salaried personnel. In general, the employees appear to be well-trained and able to perform their respective duties competently.

Risk Assessment Policies

Apple Blossom is a small company. There are no formal policies for assessing the risks that may impact the preparation of financial statements in accordance with generally accepted accounting policies. Company officers manage such risks informally. Monthly budgets are prepared for each department head. These reports are closely scrutinized, exceptions investigated, and explanations obtained for significant variances.

Information System and Control Activities

The company's accounting applications are on a local area network (LAN) using software that was purchased from a well-established software vendor. The LAN supports a number of PCs in a multi-user environment. All accounting applications are integrated, but users have access to only specific applications, controlled by means of a user ID and password. Parker Shelton, the controller, administers the LAN and has access to all accounting applications. He controls the passwords and issues them to the various accounting personnel. A user's access to the system is restricted to the specific application(s) needed to carry out the person's duties. Some employees, such as receiving clerks, have access to only specific data elements within a file.

Financial Reporting Cycle–General Ledger System

The bookkeeper, Donald McKenna, records the journal entries. Donald enters journal entries of a nonrecurring nature as the transactions occur by keying the transactions into a screen template that immediately performs an online update of the General Ledger Master File. Transactions of a similar nature (accounts payable, cash receipts, sales, and so on) are recorded in the various applications by accounting personnel using the LAN software, which produces daily registers (special journals) and reports detailing the transactions processed by each application. In addition to providing information for decision making, the daily transaction registers and reports serve as an audit trail of the transactions that have been processed against the master files in each application.

Accounts receivable transactions are processed by the accounts receivable clerk, Simon Swift. Cash receipts are maintained by the cashier, Pam Lewis, who also has access to the Accounts Receivable application module. The accounts payable (voucher) register, vendor account balances (accounts payable subsidiary ledger), and the fixed assets are maintained by the accounts payable clerk, Dave Dull. Cash disbursements are maintained by the purchasing agent, Cheryl Palmer. Payroll and sales are maintained by Donald McKenna. Anita Columbo, the inventory storeroom clerk, maintains the inventory records.

On a daily basis, Don produces a printout containing the daily transaction registers (special journals) that list the detailed transactions from each accounting application. The software also generates Journal Entry Transaction Files containing detailed journal entries, as well as printouts of these journal entries, from the following accounting applications: Sales Order Entry/Accounts Receivable, Cash Receipts, Accounts Payable, Cash Disbursements, and Payroll. Using the Journal Entry Transaction Files from each of these applications, Don updates the General Ledger Master File. Don receives approval for the journal entries from the controller, who indicates approval by initialing the journal entry printout. After receiving approval, Don processes all the Journal Entry Transaction Files, as well as any other entries. The accounting software posts the journal entries on these files to the General Ledger Master File, thereby updating the general ledger. At the end of the month, Don uses the LAN General Ledger module to prepare the trial balance and financial statements. He then gives these documents to Parker Shelton, who reviews the statements and distributes them to the president and other members of the management team.

Credit Sales System–Sales Order Entry and Accounts Receivable Processing

Customers' orders are received by the sales staff, who enter the orders via a computer screen template into the Sales Order Entry module. This program performs an online update of the Customer Master File and generates a transaction report of sales invoices by customer. (All sales are on credit.) The data in this report are accessed through the LAN by the sales manager, Ellen Jacobs, who prints out the report and indicates approval of each order by initialing the report. The computer software flags those customers whose credit limits are exceeded to preclude the processing of invoices for those customers. The Credit Manager, Brenda Robertson, may override the computer program if, in her judgment, circumstances warrant by so indicating on the sales invoice transaction report. When Ellen Jacobs and Brenda Robertson are satisfied with the sales orders, they initial the listing. The sales staff enter any necessary corrections and use a menu in the Sales Order Entry module to generate invoices from the Customer Master File. Two-part customer invoices, as well as two copies of a report listing each invoice, are generated and printed. At the time the invoices are processed, the Sales Order Entry module updates the Inventory Master File reducing the on-hand balance in each relevant Inventory Master File record.

One copy of the sales invoice report and the original (top copy) of the sales invoices are sent to Don McKenna, the bookkeeper. Once the items are shipped, Don will mail the original copy to the customers. The second printout of the sales invoice report, along with the second (stock request) copy of the invoices, are sent to the inventory storeroom clerk, Anita Columbo. Anita reviews the invoice listing for errors, such as items that according to the Sales Order Entry system were on hand, but are actually out of stock. Anita accesses the Inventory Master File records and makes corrections for any such errors noted. She then pulls the ordered items from the shelf and sends the merchandise and the invoices to the repackaging area for filling the customers' orders. (Merchandise is not back ordered; if an item is not in stock, the customer is asked to reorder at a later date.) After marking the quantities on the stock request copy, the repackaging personnel send this copy and the order to shipping. When the order is shipped to the customer, shipping personnel include the stock request copy as a packing slip. The shipping personnel also enter data from the stock request copy into the Sales Order Entry module to produce a shipping report (bill of lading) and update a data field in the Customer Master File indicating that the customer orders were shipped.

At the end of the day, the Sales Order Entry module processes a report of the items that were shipped. Donald McKenna accesses this report and sends the original copy of the invoice to the customer. Don uses the Journal Entry Transaction File generated by the Sales Order Entry module to update the General Ledger Master File (accounts receivable and sales accounts). In addition, the Sales Order Entry module automatically updates the accounts on the Customer Master File for each customer who ordered merchandise. These data are later used by the Accounts Receivable application. At the end of the day, Don prepares a billed customer report that serves as the sales register. This report is accessible on the LAN for use by Simon Swift, the accounts receivable clerk. The Accounts Receivable application includes an option allowing Simon to generate a listing of each customer's balance (accounts receivable subsidiary ledger) and a balancing report that provides a reconciliation of the accounts receivable subsidiary ledger to the general ledger accounts receivable control account. Simon Swift prepares a printout of the accounts receivable subsidiary ledger and the balancing report at the end of the day after all sales and cash receipts have been processed. He files these reports daily.

Cash Receipts

Cash collections on accounts receivable are received in the mailroom and opened by the mail clerk, Gerald Klett, who prepares a cash prelist (in triplicate) of the checks that were received. The remittance advices (mailed in by the customers), the checks, and the three copies of the prelist are routed to Simon Swift, the accounts receivable clerk. Simon enters the customer remittances into a computer screen template. The LAN software updates the Customer Master File records and produces an accounts receivable posting report, a detailed listing of the cash receipts postings. Simon sends one copy of the prelist, along with a printout of the accounts receivable posting report to the controller. Simon sends the second copy of the prelist, along with the checks and remittance advices, to the cashier, Pam Lewis. Simon retains the third copy of the prelist.

Using the Accounts Receivable module software, Pam Lewis accesses the accounts receivable posting report prepared by Simon Swift. Using the prelist, she assures that the checks were correctly posted. After correcting any posting errors, she uses a menu in the Cash Receipts module to prepare a deposit ticket (three copies) and a cash receipts journal (register) detailing the posted cash receipts transactions. She files her copy of the prelist and forwards the deposit (checks and two copies of the deposit ticket) to the treasurer, Lillian Stockton. Pam also forwards one copy of the deposit ticket to the controller, Parker Shelton, along with the cash receipts journal. Pam returns the remittance advices to Simon Swift, who files them with his copy of the prelist.

On a daily basis, Parker Shelton compares his third copy of the prelist with: the copy of the deposit ticket, the cash receipts journal from Pam Lewis, and the accounts receivable posting summary from Simon Swift. Mr. Shelton initials and files the reconciliation. He then forwards his copy of the deposit ticket to the treasurer, Lillian Stockton, who makes the deposit, retaining one copy of the deposit ticket. A validated copy of the deposit ticket is returned by the bank; Ms. Stockton uses this copy for reconciling the bank statement. At the end of the day, Don uses the Journal Entry Transaction File generated by the Cash Receipts module to update the General Ledger Master File (accounts receivable and cash accounts).

Inventory-Purchases System

After shipments are processed against the Inventory Master File records (see Credit Sales System procedures), an EOQ (economic order quantity) software routine in the Inventory-Purchases module generates an inventory reorder report, a daily listing of items requiring reorder. Cheryl Palmer, the purchasing agent, uses this report to select items for reorder. Once she has selected the items from the report, Cheryl uses the LAN Inventory-Purchases module to initiate the preparation of a purchase order. The program updates a field in each applicable Vendor Master File record to indicate the items that are on order from each selected vendor. The software also prints purchase orders in three parts, along with a report listing the purchase orders. Each purchase order is signed by the production superintendent, Theodore Brown. Cheryl sends the first copy of the purchase order to the vendor and places the second copy in the open purchase order file pending receipt of the vendor's invoice and the receiving report. Cheryl sends a copy of the purchase order report containing the on-order items to Anita Columbo, the inventory storeroom clerk. Anita is able to access the report data items on the LAN. A menu on the computer screen allows Anita to accept the data in the report and thereby update the "quantity on-order" field in each applicable Inventory Master File record.

The third copy of the purchase order is used as a receiving report. This is a blind copy (no quantities) that is sent to the receiving dock pending receipt of the merchandise. Upon receipt, the material is counted by the receiving clerks, and the quantities received are recorded on the receiving report (third) copy. The receiving personnel enter the receipts into the LAN software, which updates the "merchandise received" field in the applicable Inventory Master File records indicating that the material has been received. The module also prints a daily receiving log. The merchandise and the third copy of the purchase order are sent to the warehouse where the merchandise is counted by Anita Columbo. After verifying the receiving clerks' count and reconciling any discrepancies, Anita inputs the inventory count into a computer screen template. The LAN software updates each relevant Inventory Master File record by entering the receiving report number and increasing the quantity on hand. Any differences between the quantity received and the quantity ordered are listed on a report that is sent to Cheryl Palmer along with the third copy of the receiving report. Cheryl accesses this report from the LAN and uses it to reconcile any differences with the vendor.

Accounts Payable and Cash Disbursements

Upon receipt of the invoice from the vendor and the receiving report from the storeroom clerk, Cheryl Palmer matches these documents with the second copy of the purchase order. Cheryl sends all three documents to the accounts payable clerk, Dave Dull, who uses a menu in the Accounts Payable module to initiate an update of the Vendor Master File records; this routine computes the new balance due each vendor. The software also updates the Inventory Master File records by multiplying the new vendor inventory cost times the quantity on hand (that was entered by Anita Columbo) to yield a new inventory value. In addition, the software module prints a covering payment voucher for each vendor and produces a voucher register report listing the vouchers. After obtaining the controller's signature on each voucher, the voucher package (covering voucher, invoice, and supporting documentation) is then filed in the unpaid bills file by due date. (Any voucher not approved is backed out.) Don McKenna uses the Journal Entry Transaction File generated by the Accounts Payable module to update the General Ledger Master File (accounts payable and inventory accounts).

On a daily basis, Dave accesses a menu in the program to produce an updated accounts payable subsidiary ledger report indicating the current balance due each vendor. After the general ledger is posted, the routine produces a balancing report reconciling the subsidiary ledger to the accounts payable control account.

As vouchers are processed, the payment date in the Vendor Master File triggers the software to print a daily cash requirements report that lists those vouchers requiring payment. Dave removes those voucher packages from the unpaid bills file and sends them, along with the supporting documentation and the cash requirements report, to Cheryl Palmer. After verifying that the check amounts are correct by referencing the voucher and supporting documentation, Cheryl uses the cash requirements report and a menu in the Cash Disbursements module to initiate the preparation and printing of the checks. The software program also produces a listing of the checks. This listing is used to generate the daily cash disbursements journal (register). The Cash Disbursements module also generates a daily Journal Entry Transaction File to update the General Ledger Master File (accounts payable and cash accounts).

The voucher packages, checks, and a printout of the detailed amounts from the cash disbursements update process are forwarded to the treasurer, Lillian Stockton, who reviews the invoices and other documentation and signs the checks, along with the controller. The treasurer cancels the documents by stamping them "Paid" and sends the checks and canceled voucher packages to Dave Dull, who mails the checks to the vendors and files the canceled voucher packages.

Payroll System

Personnel records and time cards are maintained by the secretary to the president, Louise McWhorter. Notifications of hires and/or dismissals are sent to Ms. McWhorter by the various department supervisors. She then routes these notifications to Larry Lancaster for approval. For new hires, Ms. McWhorter enters the appropriate data into the LAN Payroll module, assigning the proper rate and deductions. The Payroll application creates a new Employee Master File record for each new employee entered. Louise McWhorter retains copies of this documentation for the personnel files. Weekly, the approved time cards for the hourly workers are sent to Ms. McWhorter by the various supervisors; she batches these cards and forwards them to Don McKenna. Monthly, she sends Don approved time reports for salaried personnel indicating sick days and other absences.

Don prepares the payroll by entering the time cards, time reports, and other payroll data into a computer screen template at the appropriate time. The program calculates the pay for each person, updates the Employee Master File records, and produces a payroll register containing the name, gross pay, deductions, and net pay for each employee. After having prepared the payroll, Don files the time cards and other documentation. He then sends a copy of the payroll register to Cheryl Palmer. After verifying the accuracy of the payroll, Cheryl uses the payroll register report and a menu in the Payroll module to initiate the preparation of the checks. In addition to processing the checks, the Payroll application produces a listing of the checks. This listing is used to generate the daily cash disbursements journal (register). A Journal Entry Transaction File is also produced by the Payroll module to update the General Ledger Master File (payroll expense, payroll accruals, and cash accounts). After the checks are processed, Cheryl sends the checks and a copy of the payroll register to Ms. Stockton for signature. Ms. Stockton approves the payroll by initialing the payroll register copy. After the checks are signed (by Ms. Stockton and Mr. Shelton–dual signature), they are sent to Dave Dull for distribution. Ms. Stockton files her copy of the payroll register.

Monitoring Internal Control Performance

There are no formal processes for assessing the quality of internal control performance over time. For example, Apple Blossom does not have an internal audit department. The controller, treasurer, and production supervisor closely scrutinize all financial and nonfinancial operations. In addition, the company relies on our external audit to assure that accounting policies and procedures are accurate.

Apple Blossom Cologne Company
Chart of Accounts

Each account number in the company's chart of accounts is a three-digit number. The first digit in the number is a code digit that identifies the nature of the account. The following is a listing of each code digit shown with the type of account it identifies.

1–Current assets
2–Long-term assets
3–Current liabilities
4–Long-term liabilities
5–Capital stock and other
contributed capital
6–Retained earnings and dividends
7–Revenues from operations
8–Expenses of operations
9–Nonoperating revenues and expenses

List of Account Numbers

101–Cash–Big City National Bank
102–Cash–Second National Bank
103–Petty Cash
105–Accounts receivable
106–Allowance for Bad Debts
107–Miscellaneous Receivables
109–Inventory
110–Prepaid Insurance
111–Prepaid Rent
112–Office Supplies Inventory
113–Small Tools Inventory
114–Prepaid Advertising
115–Investments in Securities
116–Allowance for Unrealized Gain/loss on
Investments (Current)

201–Long-Term Investments in Securities
202–Allowance for Unrealized Gain/loss on
Investments (Long Term)
210–Land
220–Buildings
221–Accumulated Depreciation, Buildings
230–Machinery and Equipment
231–Accumulated Depreciation, Machinery
and Equipment
240–Automotive Equipment
241–Accumulated Depreciation,
Automotive Equipment
250–Office Furniture and Fixtures
251–Accumulated Depreciation, Office
Furniture and Fixtures

301–Accounts Payable
302–Accrued Payroll Taxes
303–Wages and Salaries Payable
304–Accrued Property Taxes
305–Accrued Interest
306–Dividends Payable
307–Federal Income Taxes Payable
308–Notes Payable–Short Term
350–Lease Obligation–Short Term

401–Notes Payable–Long Term
410–Bonds Payable
411–Premium on Bonds (Notes) Payable
412–Discount on Bonds (Notes) Payable
450–Lease Obligation–Long Term

501–Common Stock
505–Other Contributed Capital
506–Unrealized Gain/loss on Investments

601–Retained Earnings
602–Appropriated Retained Earnings
605–Dividends
610—Income Summary (Current Net Income)

701–Sales
703–Sales Returns and Allowances

801–Cost of Goods Sold
820–Wage and Salary Expense
821–Payroll Tax Expense
822–Depreciation Expense

823–Rent Expense
824–Office Supplies Expense
825–Small Tools Expense
826–Advertising Expense
827–Insurance Expense
828–Repairs and Maintenance
829–Property Taxes Expense
830–Utilities Expense
831–Professional Fees
832–Miscellaneous Expense
833–Provision for Bad Debts
834–Freight-out Expense

901–Interest Expense
910–Gain/Loss on Sale of Investments
920–Income from Investments
930–Gain/Loss on Sales of Fixed Assets
940–Federal Income Tax Expense
950–Miscellaneous Income and Adjustments

Apple Blossom Cologne Company
Excerpts from Minutes--Board of Directors
December 31, 2002

Regular Meeting, January 4, 2002:

- No business of audit significance.

Regular Meeting, February 15, 2002:

- Approved 2001 annual report and authorized its release to stockholders.

Annual Meeting, February 28, 2002:

- Elected officers and approved salaries for 2002.

Chairman	Mr. James Martin	No Salary
President	Mr. Larry Lancaster	120,000
Secretary	Ms. Louise McWhorter	39,500
Other Board Members	Mr. Arthur Broman	No Salary
	Ms. Melissa Winchester	No Salary

Other salaries and wages were approved for 2002 as follows:

Theodore Brown, Production Superintendent	$83,500
Terry Freitag, Production	54,000
Cheryl Palmer, Purchasing Agent	41,900
William Beauchamp, Receiving Dock Manager	41,900
Marsha Doyle, Repackaging Area Manager	52,500
George Evershock, Shipping Dock Manager	50,300
Anita Columbo, Inventory Clerk	22,800
Ellen Jacobs, Sales Manager	77,800
Salespersons (4)	53,300
Brenda Robertson, Credit Manager	48,500
Simon Swift, Accounts Receivable Clerk	23,500
Parker Shelton, Controller	76,200
Donald McKenna, Bookkeeper	41,400
Dave Wilson, Accounts Payable Clerk	24,500
Lillian Stockton, Treasurer	78,500
Pam Lewis, Cashier	26,100
Gerald Klett, Mail Clerk	17,600

Nonsalaried positions were approved at various hourly rates.

- Appointed the law firm of Edwards, Overstreet, and Gilley as General Counsel for the year 2002.
- Appointed the CPA firm of Anderson, Olds, and Watershed as auditors for the year 2002.
- Approved construction of a garage and maintenance shop for the automotive fleet. Awarded the job to Taggart Construction Company on a bid of $33,500. } (F-2)

- Approved the disposal of the lot located at 1212
- Westminster Road. } (F-3)

Regular meeting, April 5, 2002:

- Authorized Ms. Stockton to negotiate a loan of $125,000 with the Big City National Bank. Proceeds of the loan are to be used to enter the nonflourocarbon aerosol and the pump spray markets if the results of a feasibility study prove favorable. (I-1)

Regular meeting, May 3, 2002:

- Approved purchase of GLC station wagon, $9,300.
- Approved purchase of four IBM computers at $1,095 each.
- Approved purchase of eight Kardex inventory files at $284.75 each.

(F-2)

Regular meeting, July 12, 2002:

- No business of audit significance.

Regular meeting, August 2, 2002.

- No business of audit significance.

Regular meeting, September 6, 2002:

- No business of audit significance.

Regular meeting, October 4, 2002

- Approved purchase of Atwell-Henley box-folding machine, $5,045. (F-2)

Regular meeting, November 1, 2002:

- Declined sales department request for three new automobiles.

Regular meeting, December 6, 2002:

- Authorized payment of annual dividend of $1.90 per share on January 17, 2003 to common shareholders of record on December 31, 2002. (H-3)

- Authorized Ms. Jacobs to hire two more salespersons due to increased advertising campaign and sales program.

Regular meeting, January 3, 2003:

- No business of audit significance.

Apple Blossom Cologne Company
Excerpts from Minutes--Board of Directors
December 31, 2003

Regular meeting, January 3, 2003:

- No business of audit significance.

Regular meeting, February 7, 2003:

- Approved 2002 annual report and authorized its release to stockholders.

Annual meeting, February 28, 2003:

- Elected officers and approved salaries for 2003.

Chairman	Mr. James Martin	No Salary
President	Mr. Larry Lancaster	$132,100
Secretary	Ms. Louise McWhorter	41,400
Other Board Members	Mr. Arthur Broman	No Salary
	Ms. Melissa Winchester	No Salary

Other salaries and wages were approved for 2003 as follows:

Theodore Brown, Production Superintendent	$90,300
Terry Freitag, Production Manager	56,800
Cheryl Palmer, Purchasing Agent	45,300
William Beauchamp, Receiving Dock Manager	45,300
Wayne Doyle, Repackaging Area Manager	56,700
George Evershock, Shipping Dock Manager	54,300
Anita Columbo, Inventory Clerk	24,100
Ellen Jacobs, Sales Manager	85,600
Salespersons(6) each	56,100
Brenda Robertson, Credit Manager	52,000
Simon Swift, Accounts Receivable Clerk	24,800
Parker Shelton, Controller	84,100
Donald McKenna, Bookkeeper	45,800
Dave Dull, Accounts Payable Clerk	18,600
Lillian Stockton, Treasurer	86,600
Pam Lewis, Cashier	27,600
Gerald Klett, Mail Clerk	17,900

Nonsalaried positions were approved at various hourly rates.

- Appointed the law firm of Edwards, Overstreet, and Gilley as General Counsel for the year 2003.
- Appointed the CPA firm of Anderson, Olds, Watershed as auditors for the year 2003.

Regular meeting, April 4, 2003:

- *Meeting adjourned for lack of any business needing Board's attention.*

Regular meeting, May 2, 2003:

- *Approved purchase of two forklift tractors at $11,600 each.*

Regular meeting, Jun. 6, 2003:

- *Approved purchase of a Simon-Weller pneumatic aerosol container packaging machine for $210,000.*
- *Authorized Ms. Stockton to negotiate a $475,000 loan with the Midwestern Mutual Life Insurance Company for 7 years at 10%. The loan will be used to finance a new conveyer system for the. receiving dock and new equipment. The Simon-Weller packaging machine will be pledged as collateral.*
- *Authorized Mr. Brown to finalize a lease arrangement with Fizor Leasing Corporation to lease a Holtzmann automatic spray bottle packaging machine. The lease contract specifies that Apple Blossom will lease the equipment for 10 years at a cost of $12,701 per year beginning July 1, 2003. The equipment reverts to Fizor at the termination of the lease. Total payments over the life of the lease amount to $127,010.*

Regular meeting, July 11, 2003:

- *Approved the addition of a conveyor system for the shipping dock. Awarded contract to Meyers Belts and Conveyors for their bid of $271,600. All rearrangement costs are to be capitalized.*

- *Approved the disposal of the three-ton heavy duty ceiling hoist. Authorized Mr. Freitag to seek the best possible means of disposing of the asset in light of the accident last month which left the hoist severely damaged.*

Regular meeting, August 1, 2003.

- *No business of audit significance.*

Regular meeting, September 5, 2003:

- *No business of audit significance.*

Regular meeting, October 3, 2003

- *No business of audit significance.*

Regular meeting, November 7, 2003:

- *Approved purchase of one Zorex photocopier, $8,400.*

Regular meeting, December 5, 2003:

- *Authorized payment of annual dividend of $2.50 per share on January 16, 2004 to common shareholders of record on December 31, 2003.*

Regular meeting, January 9, 2004:

- *Authorized Mr. Freitag to negotiate a contract with the McWilliams Vending and Supply Company whereby the latter would install and service food and drink vending machines in the employees' lunchroom.*
- *Authorized Mr. Brown and Ms. Jacobs to solicit and receive three bids for the purchase of a single engine, 4-passenger airplane for general use by company management and by company sales personnel.*

III
Problem Assignments

Assignment #1
Audit Planning and Integration of the Accounting Process

The first standard of field work requires that the audit work be adequately planned. Other standards stipulate that the auditor is to obtain an understanding of the company's internal control structure, including the control environment, procedures for assessing risks, control activities, the information (accounting) system, and processes for assessing the quality of internal control performance.[1] To familiarize yourself with Apple Blossom Cologne Company and to devise an overall audit strategy for the conduct of your audit examination, you have decided to develop a formal audit plan. In order to devise this plan, study the Permanent File Materials, including the following sections: *History and Background*, *Organizational Structure*, the *Internal Control* section.

The following questionnaires dealing with the control environment and the administration of the local area network (LAN) were prepared by the audit senior, Jasper Parsons, on December 15, 2003. To further your understanding of Apple Blossom's control environment, you should study the questionnaire and contemplate the implications of questions that are answered "no." You should keep these items in mind as you carry out your audit procedures.

Internal Control Questionnaire–Control Environment

		Yes	*No*	*Comments*
1.	Does management demonstrate a prudent attitude toward business risk, including an honest and sensible approach to financial reporting and meeting profits and financial goals?	√		
2.	Has the client prepared an organization chart?		√	
3.	Is there an audit committee of the board of directors?		√	
4.	Are lines of authority and the means of assigning responsibility clearly spelled out?	√		
5.	Are procedures sufficient to provide management with the ability to control the performance of company employees and effectively supervise company activities?	√		Apple Blossom is small enough that managers are able to maintain good control.
6.	Is a budget prepared for control purposes, showing variances from planned performance?		√	
7.	Are accounting procedures set out in writing?		√	

[1] Auditing standards also require the auditor to plan and perform the audit to obtain reasonable assurance that the financial statements are free of material misstatement due to fraud. See SAS 82 for specific requirements.

	Yes	No	Comments
8. Does the client maintain a chart of accounts?	√	_	
9. Are financial statements prepared periodically for submission to management?	√	_	Monthly
10. Are journal entries approved by a responsible official?	√	_	By controller who initials them.
11. Is there an internal audit function?	_	√	
12. Are personnel policies and practices adequate to ensure that competent employees are hired, that employees are trained, periodically evaluated, and adequately compensated for the responsibilities assigned?	√	_	
13. Are employees provided the resources to enable them to carry out their assigned duties?	√	_	
14. Are all personnel who have accounting responsibilities required to take annual vacations?	_	√	
15. Are employees who handle cash or similar assets bonded?	√	_	

Internal Control Questionnaire–LAN General Controls

	Yes	*No*	*Comments*
1. Is there a designated LAN administrator?	√	_	Parker Shelton, the controller, performs this function.
2. Are system administration and operations procedures documented?	√	_	
3. Are users precluded from accessing or changing LAN program source code?	√	_	The LAN uses purchased software; program source code is not accessible to users.
4. Is a standard form used to document requests for the addition, change, or deletion of LAN access capabilities?	√	_	
5. Are group or shared user IDs prohibited?	√	_	

		Yes	No	Comments
6.	Are access privileges granted on a LAN user's need to know?	√	_	User access is restricted to the specific application needed for his or her function.
7.	Are output devices in a secure area that limits access only to those authorized?	_	√	The printers are available to anyone
8.	Is the LAN server secured from unauthorized individuals?	√	_	
9.	Is critical equipment protected from theft?	√	_	
10.	Is virus checking software in use?	√	_	
11.	Is there a complete documentation of all files associated with the LAN system?	√	_	
12.	Are backup and recovery procedures documented?	√	_	
13.	Are critical files identified and backed-up?	√	_	
14.	Are backup files stored off-site?	√	_	
15.	Are users prohibited from using unlicensed software or software downloaded from unofficial sources?	√	_	
16.	Is a list of licensed software maintained for the LAN?	√	_	

Materiality

For planning purposes, your firm uses 5% of pretax income as a materiality level for determining whether the financial statements require adjustment. **The president of Apple Blossom has asked you to record all items you find requiring adjustment and you should therefore post all adjustments you find for inclusion in the financial statements. Nevertheless, you should use the 5% of pretax income amount as a reference point for planning purposes.**

Audit Planning Exercises

Complete those exercises below that have been assigned by your instructor.

1. **Engagement Letter**
The audit engagement letter is an important document that sets out the understanding between the client and the audit firm. While reviewing the Apple Blossom engagement file after Jasper Parson's departure, the partner in charge of the Apple Blossom audit discovered that Jasper had not obtained a signed engagement letter for the current year's audit. Since the engagement letter sets out the terms of the contract between the audit firm and the client, the partner is quite anxious to obtain the signed letter before you begin the audit field work. Consequently, she has asked you to prepare an engagement letter for the Apple Blossom audit.

Required. Read Part I, *General Instructions and Preparations*, and Part II, *Permanent File Materials*. Prepare an engagement letter in good form, addressing it to Mr. Larry Lancaster, President of Apple Blossom Cologne Company. Your letter should contain the following elements:

- A list of the specific services to be rendered by the firm
- An explanation of the nature of an audit engagement, as well as the limitations of an audit
- A statement that the firm will evaluate internal control and will make suggestions for improving the control structure
- The expected audit completion date
- A statement to the effect that assistance will be required from client personnel
- A statement to the effect that the completion date may have to be extended if unforeseen circumstances arise
- A statement that the firm cannot be expected to discover all fraudulent acts or other irregularities
- An indication of the basis for the fee, i.e., that the fee is based on time expended and may increase from the initial estimate if unusual circumstances are encountered.

Date the letter December 29, 2003, and sign the firm's name: Anderson, Olds, and Watershed. The letter should have a space for the signature of the person who accepts the terms of the engagement on behalf of Apple Blossom Cologne Company. Typically this would be the president or controller. There should also be a space for this person's title, as well as the date accepted. *Use word processing software.*

2. **Time Budget**
Jasper Parsons left without preparing a time budget for the audit. The partner has asked you to prepare this budget for the current year's engagement. On form P-1 are the actual hours expended in the previous year. Last year the auditors attempted to save time by cutting the hours allotted for planning and interim work. As a consequence, the audit team had to perform additional year-end work and expended a great deal of overtime due to unforeseen circumstances. These eventualities could have been avoided had the team spent more time during planning and at interim. The partner-in-charge would like to reduce the total time for this year's audit to 260 hours while avoiding the pitfalls encountered in the previous year. She believes this is possible if certain modifications are made. Specifically, planning should be increased to approximately 10% of total budgeted hours. Time spent during the interim period should be augmented to total approximately 15% of the budgeted hours, while supervision and review time should be approximately 12 - 15% of the total hours. Regarding personnel, you (the in-charge senior) will perform the bulk of the work. You will be assisted by an assistant staff auditor during certain phases of the engagement. Specifically, an assistant will: (1) perform work on operating (income statement) accounts, (2) tally the trial balance, (3) take excerpts from minutes and correspondence, (4) perform detailed work in the area of unrecorded liabilities, (5) assemble all the control weaknesses discovered during the audit, enabling you to prepare the internal control letter to management.

Required. Prepare the time budget for this year's audit by completing the *Current Year Budget* and *Percent* columns on form P-1. For those who prefer to work with spreadsheet software, use the time budget file on the ABC Working Papers diskette. (Hint: As a way of assessing the relative amount of time to be spent on each audit area, examine the current year's working trial balance. Keep in mind that certain accounts in a merchandising company are usually significant and typically present more audit risk. These accounts include Inventory, Accounts Receivable, and Accounts Payable. These accounts, as well as other larger, more material accounts appearing on the trial balance should be assigned a relatively greater proportion of the budgeted time. You should also use the prior year's working papers and the times specified for last year's budget to guide your allocation of hours for this year's audit.)

3. **Organization Chart**
Apple Blossom has not prepared a formal organization chart.

Required.
(a) Prepare an organization chart for the company. Use the information concerning administrative, accounting, and related financial responsibilities, found in the *Organizational Structure* section of the casebook, as well as other information in the Permanent File Materials. Prepare the organization chart on form P-2, or use software and label the flowchart P-2.
(b) In a separate narrative, describe any organizational changes that would improve internal control.

4. **Flowchart of Financial Reporting Cycle**
Read the narrative describing the Financial Reporting Cycle under *Accounting Process and Control Activities* found in the Internal Control section of the Permanent File Materials.

Required. Prepare a flowchart of the Financial Reporting Cycle using the captions provided on form P-3. Show the flow of transactions from each LAN application module to the preparation of the posting to the general ledger, preparation of the financial statements, and distribution of the statements. For this flowchart, start with the Journal Entry Transaction File associated with each application; show the flow to the daily updating of the general ledger, and the monthly preparation and distribution of the financial statements. Prepare the flowchart using *flowcharting software*.

5. **Analytical Procedures and Risk Analysis**
To obtain valuable information to aid in the planning effort, the auditor performs analytical procedures. Analytical procedures are used in the initial planning stages to identify matters that may require attention during the audit. Accordingly, these procedures help determine the nature, extent, and timing of audit testing. Some of the more common analytical procedures conducted during the planning phase are (1) comparison of current period financial data with those of prior periods (sometimes referred to as *common size financial statements*), (2) analysis of financial ratios, and (3) examination of the interrelationships of financial and nonfinancial information.

Required. Perform the following analytical procedures in order to gather valuable planning information. Use *spreadsheet software* to reduce your computational efforts. The 2002 and 2003 trial balances file is found on the ABC Working Papers diskette. Be sure to turn in a printout of your work:

(a) *Change Analysis.* Calculate the dollar and percentage increase or decrease in the various balance sheet and income statement account balances between the fiscal years ended 2002 and 2003. Use the following column headings:

Per Audit 12-31-02	Per Books 12-31-03	Dollar Change	Percent Change

(b) *Common Size Financial Statements.* From the figures found on the income statement working trial balance, calculate sales returns and expense accounts as a percentage of gross sales for the years 2002 and 2003. Use the following four column headings:

Per Audit 2002	2002 Percent of Gross Sales	Per Books 2003	2003 Percent of Gross Sales

(c) *Financial Ratios.* Calculate the following financial ratios to reveal any problem areas and to be able to assess the financial condition of the company.[2] (Note that net credit sales = net sales.):

	Ratio	Formula
	Liquidity Ratios	
(1)	Current ratio	$\frac{\text{current assets}}{\text{current liabilities}}$
(2)	Quick ratio	$\frac{\text{cash + net trade accounts receivable + marketable securities}}{\text{current liabilities}}$
	Activity Ratios	
(3)	Accounts receivable turnover	$\frac{\text{net credit sales}}{\text{net trade accounts receivable}}$
(4)	Days' receivables	$\frac{365}{\text{accounts receivable turnover}}$
(5)	Inventory turnover	$\frac{\text{cost of goods sold}}{\text{inventory}}$
(6)	Days' inventory	$\frac{365}{\text{inventory turnover}}$
(7)	Asset turnover	$\frac{\text{net credit sales}}{\text{total assets}}$

[2]The formulas used in these ratios comply with those found in the major financial services that report industry statistics.

Profitability Ratios

(8) Income to net worth — $\frac{\text{net income (after taxes)}}{\text{assets - liabilities}}$

(9) Income to total assets — $\frac{\text{net income (after taxes)}}{\text{total assets}}$

Leverage Ratios

(10) Liabilities to net worth — $\frac{\text{total liabilities}}{\text{assets - liabilities}}$

(11) Liabilities to total assets — $\frac{\text{total liabilities}}{\text{total assets}}$

(12) Times interest earned — $\frac{\text{net after tax income + interest expense + income taxes}}{\text{interest expense}}$

You have obtained the following median industry ratios to utilize in analyzing the results:

Ratio	*Median Industry Ratio*
Current	1.90
Quick	.90
Accounts receivable turnover	10.43
Days' receivables	35.00
Inventory turnover	5.85
Days' inventory	62.39
Asset turnover	2.83
Income to net worth	.12
Income to total assets	.05
Liabilities to net worth	1.11
Liabilities to total assets	.53
Times interest earned	3.00

Calculate the ratios on a separate part of the worksheet. Set up the formulas, entering the correct spreadsheet cells. Use the following headings:

Ratio	2002	2003	Median Industry

(d) *Analytical Procedures Memorandum.* Having carried out these analytical procedures, prepare a memorandum to assess the implications for your upcoming audit of Apple Blossom Cologne Company. *Use word processing software.* Include the following in your memorandum:

(1) *An Analysis of Audit Risks.* Relying on the results of the change analysis obtained in 5(a) and (b) above, list the accounts that appear to require attention because of significant changes. Establish and state your decision threshold for selecting accounts that should be flagged for further examination. For example, you may decide to seek explanations for changes exceeding 20% and $5,000. For each such account that you identify, provide the following possible causes for the fluctuation in the account: (1) a logical and

reasonable business reason, and (2) a possible error that may have caused the account to be misstated. In making these determinations, you should review the prior period working papers, as well as the Permanent File materials. For example, if the balance of accounts receivable is significantly higher than in the previous year, a possible error is the inclusion of January sales in December. The auditor's concern is that sales were not recorded in the correct time period. The possible effect of the error is the overstatement of sales revenue in the income statement and accounts receivable on the balance sheet. (Hint: rely on your audit text to determine the types of errors that may affect the accounts.)

(2) *Analysis of Questionable Accounts*. Discuss other accounts that may appear questionable, for example accounts that do not change when a change is expected.

(3) *Assessment of the Risk of Financial Failure.* Audit clients that are close to bankruptcy can present significant audit problems. Additionally, if sales are declining or growth has slowed, management may be inclined to manipulate the financial records. For such reasons, the auditor needs to assess the client's financial status. *Assess the financial condition of Apple Blossom Cologne Company and the consequent audit risk related to client financial failure.* Rely on the financial ratio analysis from 5(c), as well as any other information you have at hand. Refer to your finance text and other resources to determine the meaning of each of these ratios. Whenever possible, relate the ratio analysis to the change analysis in requirements 5(a) and (b). For example, if inventory turnover has slowed, relate this fact to the change in the inventory account.

(4) *Overall Appraisal of Audit Risk.* Provide an overall assessment of the audit risk associated with this engagement. Base this assessment on the analytical procedures you have performed and the knowledge of the client you gleaned from the Permanent File Materials. Assess whether Apple Blossom is a *low*, *moderate*, or *high* risk audit client. In making this determination, consider the likelihood of bankruptcy, the integrity of management, the likelihood of audit failure, and the probability of litigation stemming from this audit engagement. Explain your conclusions.

6. Assessing the Risk of Material Misstatement Due to Fraud[3]

According to generally accepted auditing standards the auditor is explicitly required to assess the risk of material misstatement in the financial statements due to fraud and is required to consider this assessment when specifying the procedures to be performed during the audit. The auditor is required to consider two types of misstatements: (1) those arising from fraudulent financial reporting, and (2) misstatements brought about by the misappropriation of assets.

Required:
Read the Permanent File materials (Section II) and the internal control questionnaires in Assignments 1-4 and 6-11. Next examine each of the risk factors listed below. Based on the permanent file materials and the questionnaires, identify each of those factors that may impact the risk of fraud in the Apple Blossom Cologne Company audit, as far as you can determine. For each factor that you so identify, comment on (1) why this factor may have a significant impact on the risk of fraud in this audit, and (2) the evidence and actions required to reduce the risk (consult appropriate auditing standards such as SAS 82, *Consideration of Fraud in a Financial Statement Audit).*

Risk Factors Relating to Misstatements Arising from Fraudulent Financial Reporting

Risk factors relating to misstatements that may arise due to fraudulent financial reporting are grouped into the following broad categories: (1) management's characteristics and influence over the control environment, (2) industry

---

[3] This section is based on *Statement on Auditing Standards 82, Consideration of Fraud in a Financial Statement Audit* (New York: American Institute of Certified Public Accountants, 1997).

conditions, and (3) the client's operating characteristics and financial stability. The first category concerns management's style and attitude related to internal control and the financial reporting process. The second category pertains to the regulatory and economic environment in which the entity operates. The third category relates to the nature and complexity of the enterprise, the types of transactions, as well as the client's financial condition and profitability. The following are specific risk factors for each of these three categories.

Risk Factors Relating to Management's Characteristics and Influence over the Control Environment

- Motivation for management to engage in fraudulent financial reporting. Specific indicators might include:
  - — A significant portion of management's compensation is represented by bonuses, stock options, or other incentives, the value of which is contingent upon the entity achieving unduly aggressive targets for operating results, financial position, or cash flow.
  - — An excessive interest by management in maintaining or increasing the entity's stock price or earnings trend through the use of unusually aggressive accounting practices.
  - — A practice by management of committing to analysts, creditors, and other third parties to achieve what appear to be unduly aggressive or clearly unrealistic forecasts.
  - — An interest by management in pursuing inappropriate means to minimize reported earnings for tax-motivated reasons.
- Failure by management to display and communicate an appropriate attitude regarding internal control and the financial reporting process. Specific indicators might include:
  - — An ineffective means of communicating and supporting the entity's values or ethics, or communication of inappropriate values or ethics. Domination of management by a single person or small group without compensating controls such as effective oversight by the board of directors or audit committee. Inadequate monitoring of significant controls.
  - — Management failing to correct known reportable conditions on a timely basis.
  - — Management setting unduly aggressive financial targets and expectations for operating personnel.
  - — Management displaying a significant disregard for regulatory authorities.
  - — Management continuing to employ an ineffective accounting, information technology, or internal auditing staff.
- Nonfinancial management's excessive participation in, or preoccupation with, the selection of accounting principles or the determination of significant estimates.
- High turnover of senior management, counsel, or board members.
- Strained relationship between management and the current or predecessor auditor. Specific indicators might include:
  - — Frequent disputes with the current or predecessor auditor on accounting, auditing, or reporting matters.
  - — Unreasonable demands on the auditor including unreasonable time constraints regarding the completion of the audit or the issuance of the auditor's reports.
  - — Formal or informal restrictions on the auditor that inappropriately limit his or her access to people or information or his or her ability to communicate effectively with the board of directors or the audit committee.
  - — Domineering management behavior in dealing with the auditor, especially involving attempts to influence the scope of the auditor's work.
- Known history of securities law violations or claims against the entity or its senior management alleging fraud or violations of securities laws.

Risk Factors Relating to Industry Conditions

- New accounting, statutory, or regulatory requirements that could impair the financial stability or profitability of the entity.
- High degree of competition or market saturation, accompanied by declining margins.
- Declining industry with increasing business failures and significant declines in customer demand.

- Rapid changes in the industry, such as high vulnerability to rapidly changing technology or rapid product obsolescence.

Risk Factors Relating to Operating Characteristics and Financial Stability

- Inability to generate cash flows from operations while reporting earnings and earnings growth.
- Significant pressure to obtain additional capital necessary to stay competitive considering the financial position of the entity–including need for funds to finance major research and development or capital expenditures.
- Assets, liabilities, revenues, or expenses based on significant estimates that involve unusually subjective judgments or uncertainties, or that are subject to potential significant change in the near term in a manner that may have a financially disruptive effect on the entity–such as ultimate collectibility of receivables, timing of revenue recognition, realizability of financial instruments based on the highly subjective valuation of collateral or difficult-to-assess repayment sources, or significant deferral of costs.
- Significant related-party transactions not in the ordinary course of business or with related entities not audited or audited by another firm.
- Significant, unusual, or highly complex transactions, especially those close to year end, that pose difficult "substance over form" questions.
- Significant bank accounts or subsidiary or branch operations in tax-haven jurisdictions for which there appears to be no clear business justification.
- Overly complex organizational structure involving numerous or unusual legal entities, managerial lines of authority, or contractual arrangements without apparent business purpose.
- Difficulty in determining the organization or individual(s) that control(s) the entity.
- Unusually rapid growth or profitability, especially compared with that of other companies in the same industry.
- Especially high vulnerability to changes in interest rates.
- Unusually high dependence on debt or marginal ability to meet debt repayment requirements; debt covenants that are difficult to maintain.
- Unrealistically aggressive sales or profitability incentive programs.
- Threat of imminent bankruptcy or foreclosure, or hostile takeover.
- Adverse consequences on significant pending transactions, such as a business combination or contract award, if poor financial results are reported.
- Poor or deteriorating financial position when management has personally guaranteed significant debts of the entity.

Risk Factors Relating to Misstatements Arising from the Misappropriation of Assets

Risk factors associated with misstatements arising from the misappropriation of assets are grouped in the two categories: (1) susceptibility of assets to misappropriation, and (2) controls. The first category pertains to the nature of an enterprise's assets and their susceptibility to theft. The second category, *controls*, involves the lack of controls designed to prevent or detect misappropriations of assets.

Risk Factors Relating to the Susceptibility of Assets to Misappropriation

- Large amounts of cash on hand or processed.
- Inventory characteristics, such as small size, high value, or high demand.
- Easily convertible assets, such as bearer bonds, diamonds, or computer chips.
- Fixed asset characteristics, such as small size, marketability, or lack of ownership identification.

Risk Factors Relating to Controls

- Lack of appropriate management oversight (for example, inadequate supervision or monitoring of remote locations).
- Lack of job applicant screening procedures relating to employees with access to assets susceptible to

misappropriation.

- Inadequate recordkeeping with respect to assets susceptible to misappropriation.
- Lack of appropriate segregation of duties or independent checks.
- Lack of appropriate system of authorization and approval of transactions (for example, in purchasing).
- Poor physical safeguards over cash, investments, inventory, or fixed assets.
- Lack of timely and appropriate documentation for transactions (for example, credits for merchandise returns).
- Lack of mandatory vacations for employees performing key control functions.

7. Planning Memorandum

Read the *General Instructions and Preparations* and the *Permanent File Materials*. Prepare a formal planning memorandum for the audit partner describing (a) each of the matters that should be considered in planning an audit (listed below as items 1-14) and (b) a description of the procedures you have carried out, or will carry out, in planning the engagement (items 15-19). Include in your memorandum a conclusion regarding the relative level of risk involved in this audit engagement. Date your memorandum January 1, 2004; assume that the December 31, 2003 trial balance is available to you. (For purposes of this memorandum, you should not include the details of specific accounting cycles or their controls.) *Use word processing software.*

Concerning the matters to consider when planning the audit, discuss the following items in your memorandum:
(1) the objective of your examination (What is the ultimate goal?)
(2) the staffing of the engagement (see Exercise 2, Time Budget)
(3) the company's pertinent aggregate financial data (for example, Total Assets)
(4) the history and background of the company
(5) the principals (owners) and their qualifications
(6) the integrity of client management
(7) the control environment
(8) capitalization (i.e., percentage of assets financed by debt and percentage financed by equity)
(9) the type of company (public/nonpublic)
(10) the markets served
(11) whether GAAP is followed
(12) materiality level for planning the audit work (use 5% of pretax income)
(13) likely audit adjustments, especially those affecting net income (see prior year's working papers)
(14) the type of opinion you expect to render.

As to the procedures you will carry out, briefly discuss the following matters:
(15) how you will familiarize yourself with the company and the industry (Internet resources? Trade journals?)
(16) what you will do regarding outsiders rendering services (e.g., attorneys)
(17) schedule of the major audit work (when work will be performed, e.g., inventory observation – see prior year's working papers)
(18) the scope and timing of audit work (if any) to be performed by the client's staff (What work did the client's staff perform during the previous audit?)
(19) the probable audit report date (see prior year's working papers).

Apple Blossom Cologne Company P-1

Time Budget

December 31, 2003

1 of 2

Audit Area	Prior Year Actual	%	Current Year Budget	%	Current Year Actual	%	Var. from Budget	Explanation of Variance from Budget
Planning	6	2.0%						
Supervision & Review	36	12.1%						
Interim:								
Cash	2	0.7%						
Accounts Receivable	2	0.7%						
Marketable Securities								
and Investments	0	0.0%						
Inventory	9	3.0%						
Prepaid Expenses	0	0.0%						
Fixed Assets	0	0.0%						
Other Assets	0	0.0%						
Accounts Payable	2	0.7%						
Accrued Liabilities	0	0.0%						
Federal Income Taxes	0	0.0%						
Notes Payable	0	0.0%						
Lease Obligations	0	0.0%						
Capital Stock	0	0.0%						
Retained Earnings	0	0.0%						
Operations	0	0.0%						
Trial Balance &								
Adjusting Entries	1	0.3%						
Total Interim	16	5.4%						
Year-end:								
Cash	30	10.1%						
Accounts Receivable	32	10.7%						
Marketable Securities								
and Investments	10	3.4%						
Inventory	32	10.7%						

Apple Blossom Cologne Company P-1

Time Budget

December 31, 2003

2 of 2

Audit Area	Prior Year Actual	%	Current Year Budget	%	Current Year Actual	%	Var. from Budget	Explanation of Variance from Budget
Prepaid Expenses	8	2.7%						
Fixed Assets	22	7.4%						
Other Assets	8	2.7%						
Accounts Payable	36	12.1%						
Accrued Liabilities	2	0.7%						
Federal Income Taxes	6	2.0%						
Notes Payable	6	2.0%						
Lease Obligations	0	0.0%						
Capital Stock	1	0.3%						
Retained Earnings	3	1.0%						
Payroll	22	7.4%						
Operations	2	0.7%						
Commitments &								
Contingencies	1	0.3%						
Minutes &								
Correspondence	2	0.7%						
Representations Letter	1	0.3%						
Unrecorded Liabilities	4	1.3%						
Report Preparation	5	1.7%						
Internal Control								
Structure Letter	6	2.0%						
In-Charge Memorandum	1	0.3%						
Other (Explain):								
Total Year-end	240	80.5%						
Total Hours	298	100.0%						

APPLE BLOSSOM COLOGNE COMPANY

P-2

Organization Chart

APPLE BLOSSOM COLOGNE COMPANY

Flowchart of Financial Reporting Cycle
(Integration of Accounting Process)

Sales Order Entry and Accts Rec. (A/R & Sales)	Cash Receipts (Cash & A/R)	Accounts Payable (A/P & Inventory)	Cash Disbursements (Cash & A/P)	Payroll (Payroll & Cash)	Bookkeeper	Controller	President, Other Managers (Monthly)

Assignment #2
Accounts Receivable and Credit Sales

The information that follows is grouped into two categories: (1) Internal Control and (2) Substantive Audit Procedures. This information is to be used to complete the exercises for this assignment. Do the optional exercises only if told to do so by your instructor.

Relevant Information

Internal Control

The following internal control questionnaire was completed by Jasper Parsons. Review this questionnaire carefully. Also, read the permanent file material describing the control environment and the accounting procedures related to the Credit Sales System. As you read this material and go through the questionnaire, keep in mind the six categories of control procedures: (1) segregation of functions, (2) access, (3) authorization, (4) input controls, (5) processing controls and (6) output controls. Then try to determine the possible errors or irregularities that could occur.

Typical errors or irregularities include:

1. Sales amounts may have been incorrectly recorded
2. Goods may have been shipped but not billed to the customer
3. Sales may have been billed to the customer but not shipped
4. Sales may have been recorded in the wrong accounting period
5. Merchandise may have been sold to customers who were bad credit risks
6. Unauthorized sales may have occurred
7. Sales may have been posted to the wrong account
8. Unauthorized write-offs of receivables may have occurred.

Internal Control Questionnaire–Credit Sales system

	Yes	*No*	*Comments*
1. Are customer subsidiary ledgers maintained by a person who has no access to cash?	_	√	Accounts receivable clerk has access to customer checks and cash prelist.
2. Are unauthorized persons unable to obtain access to customer accounts?	_	√	All LAN reports and printouts are left unlocked and are accessible to anyone. Addionally, the cashier has access to the LAN accounts receivable application.
3. Is a record maintained of accounts previously written off?	√		

4. Are credit sales approved by the credit manager before shipment? √ _

5. Are sales orders approved by the sales manager? √ _

6. Are write-offs of bad debts approved by an official not associated with the selling or credit functions? _ √ Approved by Brenda Robertson, who initials them. Credit Mgr.

7. Are credit memos approved by a responsible official? √ _ Approved by Ellen Jacobs, who initials them.

8. Are invoices prenumbered and controlled? √ _

9. Are sales invoices checked as to prices and mechanical accuracy? _ √ Client considers it not cost effective.

10. Are credit memos prenumbered and controlled? √ _

11. Are numbered shipping documents prepared for all shipments? √ _

12. Are accounts aged periodically? √ _ Monthly.

13. Are customer subsidiary ledgers reconciled with the control account periodically? √ _ Balancing report is produced by LAN software.

14. Are customers billed by someone who has no other sales or accounts receivable responsibilities? _ √ Billed by the bookkeeper, Don McKenna, who records journal entries.

Substantive Audit Procedures: Accounts Receivable and Bad Debts

To begin your substantive audit work in the accounts receivable area, you obtained an aged trial balance from Don McKenna. This schedule is included in the working papers with this assignment section referenced B-1. You may assume that you can check the aged trial balance with the accounts receivable subsidiary ledger and that the subsidiary ledger supports the aged trial balance as to both amounts due and age of accounts.

On Friday, January 2, with the client's assistance, you prepared and mailed both positive and negative accounts receivable confirmations. Positive confirmations were sent to the following seven customers with balances over $5,000: (1) Capitol Odors, (2) Darings, (3) Frankie's Floral Fragrances, (4) Incense, Inc., (5) Tears and Doefall Company, (6) Williams Fragrances, and (7) Young and Beautiful. Negative confirmations were mailed to all other customers with an accounts receivable balance. None of the confirmations was returned by the Post Office because of inability to deliver. You have received replies on all of the positive confirmations and no replies to the negative confirmations. The positive confirmations are referenced B-2 through B-5. After examining invoice #1503 you learn that the correct price was $28.30 per carton as indicated on the Incense, Inc. confirmation.

Upon checking with Brenda Robertson, you learn that a $1,748 credit should have been issued to Young and Beautiful, but the credit was never processed.

You have also discussed the accounts with Brenda Robertson, and she had the following comments about the customers and their paying habits:

Customer	*Paying Habits*
Alpha Aroma	Good account.
Bobell Beauty Supply	Extremely doubtful.
Body Bar	Slow paying, good account.
Capitol Odors	Good account.
Cut-Rate Discount Stores	Slow paying, but has always paid.
Darings	Established company, good pay.
Frankie's Floral Fragrances	Good account.
Incense, Inc.	Never been delinquent before.
Janis Dept. Store	Good account.
Lone Star Supply	Good account.
National Gas	Good account.
Rausch's Department Store	Slow pay. Good account.
Tears and Doefall	Good account.
William's Fragrances	Good account.
Young and Beautiful	$1,748 credit should be allowed.

Brenda Robertson indicated that she had spoken with both Parker Shelton, controller, and Ellen Jacobs, sales manager, about the delinquent Bobell Beauty Supplies account. They were in agreement that it should be written off. Accounts amounting to $14,760 had been written off during the year; you noted that all write-offs were approved by Ms. Robertson.

From the cash receipts journal you were able to learn of the following subsequent payments on the accounts receivables balances as of December 31, 2003.

Customer	*Payment Amount*	*Payment Date*
Body Bar	$2,850	1-07
Capitol Odors	4,300	1-09
Cut-Rate Discount Stores	2,000	1-06
Darings	26,000	1-05
Incense, Inc.	7,980	1-06
Janis Department Store	4,515	1-03
Lone Star Supply	2,500	1-08
National Gas	1,200	1-06
Rausch's Department Store	2,350	1-06
Tears and Doefall Company	59,000	1-02
Young and Beautiful	17,000	1-08

Exercises

Part A–Control Risk Analysis (Optional Exercises)

1. Using the narrative in the permanent file, as well as the information from the internal control questionnaire above, prepare an internal control systems flowchart on form P-4 for the Credit Sales System, or using software, label the form P-4. The headings have been set out for you on form P-4. Show the flow of documentation, the steps involved in the process and note any internal control features.

2. Using the flowchart, the internal control questionnaire, and the system narrative, describe the control procedures (strengths) in the system of controls over Credit Sales. For each control procedure, describe a test of controls you could perform to test the operating effectiveness of the control. Use form CSF-1. Keep in mind the six categories of control procedures: (1) segregation of duties, (2) access limited to authorized persons, (3) authorization for the proper execution of transactions, (4) input controls, (5) processing controls, and (6) output controls. Classify the strengths under these six captions.

3. For each weakness you find in the controls related to credit sales, list the weakness, a possible error or irregularity that could occur because of the weakness, and a compensating substantive test of transactions or balances to detect the error or irregularity, assuming the necessary records and documents are available to you. Use form CWF-1. Classify the weaknesses under the six categories of control procedures as outlined in (2) above. You should keep these weaknesses in mind, as well as the five financial statement assertions when you write the substantive audit steps in your programs.

4. ALTERNATIVE A
   Prepare an audit program consisting of tests of controls to test internal control strengths. Utilize the analysis of strengths you have prepared to guide you, remembering to keep the internal control objectives and financial statement assertions in mind. Write your test of controls audit program on form SP-1.

   ALTERNATIVE B
   Prepare a system audit program for the Credit Sales System consisting of: (1) tests of controls to test the control procedures; (2) substantive tests of details of transactions; and/or (3) dual-purpose tests having both test of controls and substantive aspects. Utilize the analysis of strengths and weaknesses you have prepared to guide you, remembering to keep internal control objectives and the financial statement assertions in mind. Write your system audit program on form SP-1. Use the headings: Tests of Controls, Dual-Purpose Tests, and Substantive Tests of Transactions. List the appropriate audit steps under each of these headings.

   Note: When analyzing internal control by working the optional exercises in this assignment, identify the audit program step that addresses the strength or weakness in internal control by cross-referencing the program step to each strength with an "S" and each weakness with a "W" (e.g., S-1, S-2, W-1, W-2, etc.).

PART B–Attributes Sampling Exercise (Optional Exercise)

You have decided to conduct a test of controls using attributes sampling methods to determine the extent to which sales invoices are supported by a shipping document. There should be a shipping document for each sales invoice. During the year, Apple Blossom issued 468 sales invoices, numbered 20099 to 20566.

invoice. During the year, Apple Blossom issued 468 sales invoices, numbered 20099 to 20566.

You have decided that for purposes of this test that the tolerable deviation rate should be 4% with an expected population deviation rate of 0% and an acceptable risk of assessing control risk too low of .05 (the risk of assessing control risk too low is also known as *the acceptable risk of overreliance* or ARO). Use the tables provided with the materials at the end of this assignment to determine the sample size. According to the Anderson, Olds, and Watershed audit manual, a small population such as this one should be reduced using the following finite correction factor:

$$n = \frac{n'}{1 + n' / N}$$

where n' = sample size obtained from the table
N = population size
n = corrected sample size.

Required:

1. State the objective of the test.
2. Specify the attribute and the exception condition.
3. Define the population and the sampling unit.
4. Determine the appropriate sample size after applying the finite correction factor.
5. Select the invoices to be included in your sample. Use a random number table or spreadsheet software to generate random numbers (e.g., in EXCEL, use Random Number Generation under Tools, Data Analysis) for this purpose.
6. Assume that you examine each invoice selected. During 2003, Apple Blossom issued 468 sales invoices, numbered 20099 to 20566. Regarding shipping documents, this population of sales invoices has the following characteristics: 437 invoices are supported by shipping documents. The following thirty-one invoices are not supported by a shipping document:

20100	20178	20310	20364	20487	20552
20112	20209	20321	20381	20497	
20121	20232	20324	20391	20510	
20143	20240	20329	20399	20522	
20149	20261	20333	20412	20439	
0155	20298	20357	20418	20542	

(Of course the auditor would not actually have this information regarding errors in the population. Use it, however, to evaluate the results of your sample by identifying those invoices in your sample with a deviation.)

7. Based on the number of deviations you have found in your sample, state the sample error rate and the achieved upper error rate using the evaluation table provided in this assignment.
8. State your conclusion. If you conclude that controls are not operating effectively, state the compensating substantive test(s) that you would perform.

Use the attributes sampling tables included with the material at the end of this assignment to determine the sample size and evaluate results. Consult your textbook for information on attributes sampling. Guidance is also provided in the AICPA Auditing Practice Release, *Audit Sampling*, pp. 17-33 (AICPA 1999).

PART C–Required Exercises: Substantive Procedures

1. Prepare a substantive audit program to test accounts receivable balances and bad debts. The construction of such a program should begin with an explicit recognition of the five financial statement assertions: (1) existence or occurrence, (2) completeness, (3) rights and obligations, (4) valuation or allocation, and (5) presentation and disclosure. You should derive your specific audit objectives for accounts receivable and bad debts from these assertions. Your audit program should address the five financial statement assertions, as well as any weaknesses in the control structure that you have uncovered. In this regard, keep in mind the six categories of control procedures, as well as the other control structure elements. You may assume that you have satisfied yourself as to any assertions not specifically mentioned in the narrative.

   As you write your program, remember the generalized evidence-gathering procedures of (1) recalculation, (2) physical observation, (3) confirmation, (4) verbal inquiry, (5) vouching of documents, (6) tracing, (7) scanning, and (8) analytical procedures. Use them to help you write the specific evidence-gathering procedures in your program. Write your audit program on form AP-1. Use the financial statement assertions as the major headings or captions for your program. List the appropriate steps under each of these headings.

   Note: As you go through the audit, whenever you prepare an audit program to test the substantive details of balances, identify the program step that addresses the weakness in internal control by referencing the appropriate question from the internal control questionnaire (e.g., Q-1, Q-2, etc.). If you have conducted a formal analysis of internal control by having worked the optional exercises, then you should cross-reference your program steps to the relevant weaknesses you have identified (W-1, W-2, and so on).

2. Study the prior year working papers, schedules B-1 through B-5. Note the use of "tick marks" to evidence the audit work and the system of cross-referencing the working papers. Perform all required audit work on the current year's schedules B-1 through B-5 and prepare schedule B-6 to analyze the allowance account for the current year, performing all appropriate audit work. You have determined that the expected uncollectible percentages from the prior year are still appropriate for the current year.

P-4

APPLE BLOSSOM COLOGNE COMPANY

Credit Sales System

Sales	Credit Manager	Stores (Warehouse/Repack)	Shipping	Bookkeeper	Accounts Receivable Clerk

APPLE BLOSSOM COLOGNE COMPANY

Credit Sales System
Internal Control Strengths

Strength	Possible Test of Controls

APPLE BLOSSOM COLOGNE COMPANY CWF-1

Credit Sales System
Internal Control Weaknesses

Weakness	Potential Error	Compensating Substantive Procedure

APPLE BLOSSOM COLOGNE COMPANY SP-1

Credit Sales
Program

STATISTICAL SAMPLING TABLES

Statistical Sample Sizes for Test of Controls—5 Percent Risk of Assessing Control Risk Too Low (with number of expected errors in parentheses)

Expected Population Deviation Rate	*Tolerable Rate*										
	2%	*3%*	*4%*	*5%*	*6%*	*7%*	*8%*	*9%*	*10%*	*15%*	*20%*
0.00%	149(0)	99(0)	74(0)	59(0)	49(0)	42(0)	36(0)	32(0)	29(0)	19(0)	14(0)
.25	236(1)	157(1)	117(1)	93(1)	78(1)	66(1)	58(1)	51(1)	46(1)	30(1)	22(1)
.50	*	157(1)	117(1)	93(1)	78(1)	66(1)	58(1)	51(1)	46(1)	30(1)	22(1)
.75	*	208(2)	117(1)	93(1)	78(1)	66(1)	58(1)	51(1)	46(1)	30(1)	22(1)
1.00	*	*	156(2)	93(1)	78(1)	66(1)	58(1)	51(1)	46(1)	30(1)	22(1)
1.25	*	*	156(2)	124(2)	78(1)	66(1)	58(1)	51(1)	46(1)	30(1)	22(1)
1.50	*	*	192(3)	124(2)	103(2)	66(1)	58(1)	51(1)	46(1)	30(1)	22(1)
1.75	*	*	227(4)	153(3)	103(2)	88(2)	77(2)	51(1)	46(1)	30(1)	22(1)
2.00	*	*	*	181(4)	127(3)	88(2)	77(2)	68(2)	46(1)	30(1)	22(1)
2.25	*	*	*	208(5)	127(3)	88(2)	77(2)	68(2)	61(2)	30(1)	22(1)
2.50	*	*	*	*	150(4)	109(3)	77(2)	68(2)	61(2)	30(1)	22(1)
2.75	*	*	*	*	173(5)	109(3)	95(3)	68(2)	61(2)	30(1)	22(1)
3.00	*	*	*	*	195(6)	129(4)	95(3)	84(3)	61(2)	30(1)	22(1)
3.25	*	*	*	*	*	148(5)	112(4)	84(3)	61(2)	30(1)	22(1)
3.50	*	*	*	*	*	167(6)	112(4)	84(3)	76(3)	40(2)	22(1)
3.75	*	*	*	*	*	185(7)	129(5)	100(4)	76(3)	40(2)	22(1)
4.00	*	*	*	*	*	*	146(6)	100(4)	89(4)	40(2)	22(1)
5.00	*	*	*	*	*	*	*	158(8)	116(6)	40(2)	30(2)
6.00	*	*	*	*	*	*	*	*	179(11)	50(3)	30(2)
7.00	*	*	*	*	*	*	*	*	*	68(5)	37(3)

* Sample size is too large to be cost-effective for most audit applications.
Note: This table assumes a large population. For discussion of the effect of population size on sample size, see chapter 3.

Statistical Sampling Results Evaluation Table for Tests of Controls—Upper Limits at 5 Percent Risk of Assessing Control Risk Too Low

Sample Size	*Actual Number of Deviations Found*										
	0	*1*	*2*	*3*	*4*	*5*	*6*	*7*	*8*	*9*	*10*
25	11.3	17.6	*	*	*	*	*	*	*	*	*
30	9.5	14.9	19.6	*	*	*	*	*	*	*	*
35	8.3	12.9	17.0	*	*	*	*	*	*	*	*
40	7.3	11.4	15.0	18.3	*	*	*	*	*	*	*
45	6.5	10.2	13.4	16.4	19.2	*	*	*	*	*	*
50	5.9	9.2	12.1	14.8	17.4	19.9	*	*	*	*	*
55	5.4	8.4	11.1	13.5	15.9	18.2	*	*	*	*	*
60	4.9	7.7	10.2	12.5	14.7	16.8	18.8	*	*	*	*
65	4.6	7.1	9.4	11.5	13.6	15.5	17.4	19.3	*	*	*
70	4.2	6.6	8.8	10.8	12.6	14.5	16.3	18.0	19.7	*	*
75	4.0	6.2	8.2	10.1	11.8	13.6	15.2	16.9	18.5	20.0	*
80	3.7	5.8	7.7	9.5	11.1	12.7	14.3	15.9	17.4	18.9	*
90	3.3	5.2	6.9	8.4	9.9	11.4	12.8	14.2	15.5	16.8	18.2
100	3.0	4.7	6.2	7.6	9.0	10.3	11.5	12.8	14.0	15.2	16.4
125	2.4	3.8	5.0	6.1	7.2	8.3	9.3	10.3	11.3	12.3	13.2
150	2.0	3.2	4.2	5.1	6.0	6.9	7.8	8.6	9.5	10.3	11.1
200	1.5	2.4	3.2	3.9	4.6	5.2	5.9	6.5	7.2	7.8	8.4

* Over 20 percent
Note: This table presents upper limits as percentages. This table assumes a large population.

Substantive Audit Program–Accounts Receivable and Bad Debts

Assertions

Begin with the list of assertions below and add others you think appropriate. Then write your audit program to test those assertions.

1. None of the accounts receivable are fictitious.
2. No accounts receivable have been omitted from the balance sheet.
3. The accounts receivable are collectible in the normal course of business.
4. The accounts receivable are bona fide claims owed the company.
5. Pledged accounts receivable or accounts receivable used as collateral are disclosed.
6. Receivables from directors, officers, and affiliates are separately disclosed.

Program Steps

Apple Blossom Cologne Company B-1

Accounts Receivable - Aged Trial Balance

12-31-03

(Prepared by Client)

Customer	Current 1-30 days	30-60 Days	60-90 Days	Over 90 Days	Total	Confirmation Mailed 1-2-04	Subsequent Collection to 1-15-04	Comments by Credit Manager–B. Robertson
Alpha Aroma		3900			3900			
Bobell Beauty Supplies				750	750			
Body Bar	2100	800	1050		3950			
Capitol Odors	7400				7400			
Cut-Rate Discount Stores	2380	1720	400		4500			
Darings	26200	5500			31700			
Frankies Floral Frag.	17200				17200			
Incense, Inc.	1760	7300			9060			
Janis Department Stores	4600				4600			
Lone Star Supply	3290				3290			
National Gas	1850				1850			
Rausch's Dept.Store	2700	1350			4050			
Tears & Doefall Company	77540				77540			
William's Fragrances	19400				19400			
Young & Beautiful	17000		1748		18748			
Various Other Acct's.	4767				4767			
	188187	20570	3198	750	212705			

B- 2

January 2, 2004

Frankie's Floral Fragrances
602 River Street
Chicago, Illinois 60617

Dear Sir or Madam:

For the purpose of providing independent confirmation of our accounts receivable, please advise our auditors, Anderson, Olds, and Watershed, Certified Public Accountants, of the correctness of your balance with us as of December 31, 2003, as shown on the enclosed statement.

After comparing the statement with your records, please sign the confirmation below and return it directly to our auditors in the enclosed, addressed envelope. If your records differ from the balance shown, please note your **exceptions** below.

This letter is *not* a request for payment, but merely for confirmation of your account balance.

Very truly yours,
APPLE BLOSSOM COLOGNE COMPANY

By ___Parker Shelton___

CONFIRMATION OF ACCOUNTS RECEIVABLE

Confirmation Request No. 1___

Anderson, Olds, and Watershed
Certified Public Accountants
615 Big City National Bank Building
Main at Michigan Avenue
Chicago, Illinois 60612

Dear Sir or Madam:

The statement of our account showing a balance of $___17,200___ as of ___12/31/03___ is correct except as noted below.

Very truly yours,
Frankie's Floral Fragrances
James Whitmore
Chief Accountant

Date January 19, 2004

Exceptions:

No exceptions

CONFIRMATION OF ACCOUNTS RECEIVABLE

Confirmation Request No. 2

Anderson, Olds, and Watershed
Certified Public Accountants
615 Big City National Bank Building
Main at Michigan Avenue
Chicago, Illinois 60612

Dear Sir or Madam:

The statement of our account showing a balance of $ 19,400 as of 12/31/03 is correct except as noted below.

Very truly yours,
William's Fragrances
William Brown

Date 1/16/04

Exceptions:
None

CONFIRMATION OF ACCOUNTS RECEIVABLE

Confirmation Request No. 3

Anderson, Olds, and Watershed
Certified Public Accountants
615 Big City National Bank Building
Main at Michigan Avenue
Chicago, Illinois 60612

Dear Sir or Madam:

The statement of our account showing a balance of $ 77,540 as of 12/31/03 is correct except as noted below.

Very truly yours,
Tears and Doefall Company
William Okeefe
Controller

Date January 14, 2004

Exceptions:
$59,000 payment was made prior to 12/31/03. The balance should only be $18,540. Please correct your records

---

CONFIRMATION OF ACCOUNTS RECEIVABLE

Confirmation Request No. 4

Anderson, Olds, and Watershed
Certified Public Accountants
615 Big City National Bank Building
Main at Michigan Avenue
Chicago, Illinois 60612

Dear Sir or Madam:

The statement of our account showing a balance of $ 31,700 as of 12/31/03 is correct except as noted below.

Very truly yours,
Darings
Rosmary Williams
Head Bookkeeper

Date January 20, 2004

Exceptions:
Balance is wrong. We only owe $5,700.

CONFIRMATION OF ACCOUNTS RECEIVABLE

Confirmation Request No. 5

Anderson, Olds, and Watershed
Certified Public Accountants
615 Big City National Bank Building
Main at Michigan Avenue
Chicago, Illinois 60612

Dear Sir or Madam:

The statement of our account showing a balance of $ 18,748 as of 12/31/03 is correct except as noted below.

Very truly yours,
Young and Beautiful
Roger McAdams
President

Date January 12, 2004

Exceptions:
The correct balance is $17,000. There was $1,748 in damage to an October shipment. We have been promised credit on that order and I refuse to pay it!

CONFIRMATION OF ACCOUNTS RECEIVABLE

Confirmation Request No. 6

Anderson, Olds, and Watershed
Certified Public Accountants
615 Big City National Bank Building
Main at Michigan Avenue
Chicago, Illinois 60612

Dear Sir or Madam:

The statement of our account showing a balance of $ 7,400 as of 12/31/03 is correct except as noted below.

Very truly yours,
Capitol Odors
Onita Sawyer
Bookkeeper

Date 1/12/04

Exceptions:
No exceptions

CONFIRMATION OF ACCOUNTS RECEIVABLE

Confirmation Request No. 7

Anderson, Olds, and Watershed
Certified Public Accountants
615 Big City National Bank Building
Main at Michigan Avenue
Chicago, Illinois 60612

Dear Sir or Madam:
The statement of our account showing a balance of $ 9,060 as of 12/31/03 is correct except as noted below.

Very truly yours,
Incense, Inc.
Zeke Glutz
Controller

Date January 15, 2004

Our balance is not correct. The shipment for invoice #1503 received 12/23/03 is in error. We ordered 20 cartons of Sumptuous Lemon at $28.30 per carton but were charged $82.30 per carton. We demand a credit of $1080.

Assignment #3
Cash

The information that follows is grouped into two categories: 1) Internal Control and 2) Substantive Audit Procedures. This information is to be used to complete the exercises for this assignment. Do the optional exercises only if told to do so by your instructor.

Relevant Information

Internal Control

The Apple Blossom Cologne Company has two bank checking accounts. The general account (account number 101) is with the Big City National Bank, Main at Michigan Avenue, Chicago, Illinois. It is used for ordinary cash receipts and disbursements transactions. The payroll account (102) is with the Second National Bank, 615 Lakeway Road, Chicago, Illinois. The payroll account is not an imprest account and transfers between it and the general account occur frequently. All transfers are journalized through the cash receipts journal.

The following internal control questionnaire pertaining to cash receipts, cash disbursements, and cash balances was completed by Jasper Parsons on December 15, 2003. Review this questionnaire carefully along with the Permanent File material describing the control environment, as well as the accounting and control procedures related to the various cash subsystems. Your firm has found that personnel involved in this area are generally competent.

As you read this material and analyze the internal control questionnaire, keep in mind the six control procedure categories: (1) segregation of duties, (2) access, (3) authorization, (4) input controls, (5) processing controls, and (6) output controls. Then consider possible errors or irregularities that could occur in the accounting system related to cash transactions and balances.

Typical errors or irregularities involving cash receipts, disbursements, and balances include:

Cash Receipts

1. Cash receipts may have been deposited in the bank but not recorded in the cash receipts journal.
2. Cash receipts may have been recorded but not deposited in the bank.
3. The receipt may have been credited to the wrong account.
4. The amount of cash receipts may have been incorrectly recorded.
5. Cash receipts may have been recorded in the wrong accounting period.
6. Transfers of cash among bank accounts may have been recorded incorrectly.

Cash Disbursements

1. Unauthorized disbursements may have occurred.
2. Disbursements may have been recorded but the check not mailed.
3. Disbursements may have been made but not recorded in the cash disbursements journal.
4. The disbursement may have been recorded in the wrong account.
5. Disbursements may have been recorded in the wrong accounting period.
6. Disbursements related to interbank transfers may have been incorrectly recorded.

Cash Balances

1. The bank reconciliation may have been purposefully misfooted to cover a defalcation.
2. The reconciliation may include fictitious deposits in transit.
3. Outstanding checks may have been omitted from the reconciliation to conceal a cash shortage.

Internal Control Questionnaire–Cash Transactions and Balances

Cash Receipts

Probably the most important control over cash receipts is the preparation of an independent record of those receipts for later reconciliation with the recorded accountability.

	Yes	*No*	*Comments*
1. Are all mail receipts recorded for control purposes?	√	_	
2. Does the person who opens the mail record the receipts immediately?	√	_	Opened by G. Klett, the mail clerk, who repares prelist.
3. Are the mail receipts listed by a person who has no other cash or accounts receivable responsibilities?	√	_	
4. Is the list of mail receipts independently reconciled to the accounting records by a person who does not have access to cash receipts?	√	_	By controller who initials reconciliation.
5. Are bank deposits made by a person who does not prepare the deposit?	√	_	
6. Are the duties of the cashier separate from those of the accounts receivable clerk?	_	√	Accounts receivable clerk has access to checks & prelist. Cashier has access to A/R LAN application.
7. Is a duplicate deposit ticket received by someone who does not prepare or make the deposit?	_	√	Received by treasurer, who makes deposit and reconciles bank statement.
8. Are receipts deposited intact daily?	_	√	Deposited intact but not always daily.

Cash Disbursements

	Yes	No	*Comments*
1. Are check signers independent of persons who approve cash disbursements?	_	√	Controller signs checks and approves vouchers for payment.
2. Are check signers independent of persons who post to the general ledger?	_	√	Controller signs checks and also approves journal entries.
3. Are check signers authorized by the board of directors?	√	_	
4. Are dual signatures utilized?	√	_	
5. Are prenumbered checks used?	√	_	
6. Are voided checks properly mutilated and retained?	√	_	
7. Are all disbursements made by check except petty cash disbursements?	√	_	
8. Are blank checks properly controlled?	_	√	The checks are left unlocked.

Cash Balances

	Yes	No	*Comments*
1. Are bank accounts reconciled on a monthly basis?	√	_	
2. Are bank statements sent directly to the person who reconciles the bank account?	√	_	
3. Are bank accounts reconciled by a person who has no other cash responsibilities?	_	√	Reconciled by treasurer.

Substantive Audit Procedures: Cash Balances

Lillian Stockton, the treasurer, prepares monthly bank reconciliations for both bank accounts. Don McKenna provided you with a copy of the reconciliations for each bank for the month of December, 2003. You also obtained from Don selected portions of the cash receipts and cash disbursements journals. You have received directly from the banks the confirmations and cutoff bank statements that were requested January 2, 2004. The cutoff bank statements cover the period from January 1 to January 12, 2004.

On December 31, 2003, you were on the client's premises for the purpose of counting any undeposited cash receipts and the petty cash fund at year-end. The cashier, Pam Lewis, prepares the company bank deposits. However, on December 31, 2003, she did not prepare a deposit, so you obtained the undeposited cash receipts from her, listed your count, and returned the funds to her, obtaining a receipt for their return. Pam also has charge of the petty cash fund. You obtained control of it, counted it, recorded your count, and returned it to Pam, obtaining a receipt for its return. Working papers for these cash counts, A-6 and A-7, respectively, are included in the working paper schedules provided.

The cutoff bank statement, along with items clearing during the cutoff period, which you requested from Big City National Bank, are shown in Exhibit 1. The cutoff statement and the clearings for the Second National Bank are shown in Exhibit 2. A selected portion of the cash receipts journal is provided as Exhibit 3, while a selected portion of the cash disbursements journal is shown in Exhibit 4. You may assume that checks written in December and not shown as clearing on the cutoff bank statement cleared on the December bank statement.

The following is a listing, by working paper index, of the working papers (a) prepared for you by the client, (b) obtained directly from the banks, and (c) prepared by you when counting petty cash and undeposited cash receipts. They are included for your use in this assignment.

	Reference
Bank reconciliation–Big City National Bank	A-1
Standard bank confirmation–Big City National Bank	A-2
Bank Reconciliation–Second National Bank	A-3
Standard bank confirmation–Second National Bank	A-4
Undeposited cash receipts–Big City National Bank	A-6
Petty cash fund	A-7

Exercises

PART A–Control Risk Analysis (Optional Exercises)

1. Using the narrative in the Permanent File, as well as the information from the internal control questionnaire above, prepare an internal control systems flowchart for the Cash Receipts: Collections on Account system. Use form P-5 or software and label the flowchart P-5. The headings have been provided for you on this form. Show the flow of documentation, the steps involved in the process, and note any internal control features.

2. (a) Describe the control procedures (strengths) in the system of controls over cash receipts. For each strength, describe a test of controls you could perform to test the operating effectiveness of the strength. Classify your strengths according to the six categories of control procedures (see General Instructions and Preparations). Use form CSF-2.
(b) For each weakness you discover in the controls related to cash receipts, list the weakness, a potential error or irregularity, and a compensating substantive test of transactions or balances that could detect the error or irregularity, assuming the necessary records and documents are available to you. Use form CWF-2. Classify the weaknesses according to the six control procedure categories. You should keep these weaknesses in mind while you write the substantive audit steps in your programs.

3. Prepare a system audit program for the Cash Receipts System consisting of: (1) tests of controls to test the control procedures (strengths); (2) substantive tests of details of transactions; and/or (3) dual-purpose tests having both test of control and substantive aspects. Utilize the analysis of strengths and weaknesses you have prepared to guide you, remembering to keep the financial statement assertions in mind. (Example:

"All cash receipts have been recorded.") Utilize form SP-2. Use three headings: Tests of Controls, Dual-Purpose Tests, and Substantive Tests of Transactions.

4. (a) Describe the control procedures (strengths) related to cash disbursements and cash balances. For each strength, describe a test of controls you could perform to test the operating effectiveness of the control. Use form CSF-3. Classify the strengths according to the six control procedure categories.

   (b) For each weakness you find in the controls related to cash disbursements and balances, list the weakness, a potential error or irregularity, and a compensating substantive test of transactions or balances that could detect the error or irregularity, assuming the necessary records and documents are available to you. Use form CWF-3. Classify the weaknesses according to the six control categories. These weaknesses should be kept in mind as you write the substantive audit steps in your programs.

5. Prepare a system program for the Cash Disbursements System consisting of tests of controls and substantive tests of details of transactions. Keep the financial statement assertions in mind. Your program may contain dual-purpose tests, having both test of controls and substantive aspects. Use form SP-3. Your headings should be as follows: Tests of Controls, Dual-Purpose Tests, and Substantive Tests of Transactions.

PART B–Required Exercises: Substantive procedures

1. Prepare a substantive audit program to test cash balances. The construction of such a program should begin with the five financial statement assertions: (1) existence or occurrence, (2) completeness, (3) rights and obligations, (4) valuation or allocation, and (5) presentation and disclosure. You should derive your specific audit objectives for cash balances from these assertions. Your audit program should address the five financial statement assertions, as well as any weaknesses you have uncovered in the internal control structure. In this regard, keep in mind the six control procedure categories, as well as the other control structure elements. You may assume that you have satisfied yourself as to any assertions not specifically mentioned in the narrative.

   As you write your program, remember the generalized evidence-gathering procedures of (1) recalculation, (2) physical observation, (3) confirmation, (4) verbal inquiry, (5) vouching of documents, (6) tracing, (7) scanning, and (8) analytical procedures. Use them to help you write the specific evidence-gathering procedures in your program. Write your program on form AP-2. Use the financial statement assertions as the major headings, or captions, for your program.

2. Study the prior year's working papers, paying attention to the use of tick marks to indicate your audit procedures, and the system of cross-referencing among working papers.

   Gather evidence as necessary from the exhibits, the direct bank mailings, the client-prepared schedules, and your own observations to perform your audit work in the cash area by completing working papers A-1 through A-7. Prepare schedule A-5 analyzing the propriety of interbank transfers.

P-5

APPLE BLOSSOM COLOGNE COMPANY

Cash Receipts System: Collections on Account

Mailroom Clerk	Accounts Receivable Clerk	Cashier	Controller	Treasurer

Cash Receipts System
Internal Control Strengths

Strength	**Possible Test of Controls**

APPLE BLOSSOM COLOGNE COMPANY **CWF-2**

Cash Receipts System
Internal Control Weaknesses

Weakness	Potential Error	Compensating Substantive Procedure

Cash Receipts System
Program

APPLE BLOSSOM COLOGNE COMPANY CSF-3

Cash Disbursements and Balances
Internal Control Strengths

<u>Strength</u>	<u>Possible test of Controls</u>

APPLE BLOSSOM COLOGNE COMPANY CWF-3

Cash Disbursements and Balances
Internal Control Weaknesses

Weakness	Potential Error	Compensating Substantive Procedure

Cash Disbursements System
Program

Substantive Audit Program–Cash Balances

Assertions

Begin with the list of assertions below and add others as you think appropriate. Then write your audit program to test those assertions.

1. The amount of cash is not materially more than the amount shown on the balance sheet.
2. All cash has been recorded.
3. Cash is correctly shown as a current asset.
4. Cash is not restricted to noncurrent use.

Program Steps

EXHIBIT 1

BIG CITY NATIONAL BANK
Cutoff Bank Statement and Clearings

BIG CITY NATIONAL BANK

Main at Michigan Avenue
Chicago, Illinois 60612

Statement of Account #146-2013

APPLE BLOSSOM COLOGNE COMPANY

DATE	CHECKS			DEPOSITS		BALANCE
12-31-03	Balance forward					816,660
1-2-04	135	821	650	45,987	59,000	920,041
1-5-04	350	26,000	75,000	12,594	30515	861,800
1-6-04	10,000			13,530		865,330
1-7-04	744			2,850		867,436
1-8-04	1,100			19,500		885,836
1-9-04	468	8,400	620	4,300		880,648
1-12-04	240	109,120	4820			766,468

EXHIBIT 1 (Continued)

Deposit slips that agree with the above statement were received with the cutoff bank statement. The following is a list of paid checks that were received with the cutoff bank statement.

Check Number	Date of Check	Cleared Bank	Payee	Amount
1443	12-24	1-02	Alex McBane Heating	650
1446	12-24	1-02	Longhorn Garbage Disposal	135
1449	12-27	1-02	DeBella Hardware	821
1452	12-31	1-05	Second National Bank	26,000
1445	12-24	1-05	Office Decorators	350
1453	1-02	1-05	Second National Bank	75,000
1451	12-30	1-06	Second National Bank	10,000
1450	12-30	1-07	Quick Print Printers	744
1454	1-05	1-08	Central Power & Light	1,100
1456	1-06	1-09	Hart Murphy Office Outfitters	8,400
1455	1-05	1-09	William F. Reimann	468
1457	1-06	1-09	Fulton Paper Co.	620
1462	1-09	1-12	Edwards, Overstreet, & Gilley	4,820
1461	1-08	1-12	Fruit Juicy Perfume Company	109,120
1458	1-07	1-12	Hoffmann Supply Company	240

EXHIBIT 2

SECOND NATIONAL BANK
Cutoff Bank Statement and Clearings

SECOND NATIONAL BANK

615 Lakeway Road
Chicago, Illinois 60612

Statement of Account #36-118-402

APPLE BLOSSOM COLOGNE COMPANY

DATE	CHECKS		DEPOSITS		BALANCE
12-31-03	Balance forward				2,812
1-2-04	1,844		10,000	26,000	36,968
			75,000		111,968
1-5-04	39,705	3,190			69,073
1-6-04	55,586	2,950			10,537
1-7-04					10,537
1-8-04					10,537
1-9-04					10,537
1-12-04	1,758				8,779

EXHIBIT 2 (Continued)

Deposit slips that agree with the above statement were received with the cutoff bank statement. The following is a list of paid checks that were received with the cutoff bank statement.

Check Number	Date of Check	Cleared Bank	Payee	Amount
6889,6893,6897 6899	12-26	1-02	4 hourly employees (see cash disb. journal for names)	$1,844
6904,6906,6907 6910,6911,6913 6914,6916,6919 6925	1-02	1-05	10 salaried employees	39,705
6927,6929,6931 6932,6936,6939 6940	1-02	1-05	7 hourly employees	3,190
6903,6905,6908 6909,6912,6915 6917,6918,6920 6921,6922,6923 6924,6926	1-02	1-06	14 salaried employees	55,586
6928,6930,6933 6934,6935,6937 6938	1-02	1-06	7 hourly employees	2,950
6943,6947,6949 6950	1-09	1-12	4 hourly employees	1,758

EXHIBIT 3

CASH RECEIPTS JOURNAL
(selected portion)

CASH DEBIT				CREDIT	
BIG CITY NATIONAL	SECOND NAT.	DATE	SOURCE	ACCOUNTS RECEIVABLE	OTHER
163,093	-0-	12-24-03	Total brought forward	163,093	-0-
25,800		12-24	Various A/R - Listed	25,800	
45,987		12-29	Various A/R - Listed	45,987	
	10,000	12-30	Big City National Bank		10,000*
	26,000	12-31	Big City National Bank		26,000**
12,594		12-31	Various A/R - Listed	12,594	
247,474	36,000	12-31-03	December totals	247,474	36,000
-0-	-0-	1-01-04	Beginning balance	-0-	-0-
59,000		1-02	Tears and Doefall Co.	59,000	
	75,000	1-02	Big City National Bank		75,000**
30,515		1-05	Various A/R - Listed	30,515	
13,530		1-06	Various A/R - Listed	13,530	
2,850		1-07	Body Bar	2,850	
19,500		1-08	Various A/R - Listed	19,500	
3,750		1-08	Sears Credit Corp.		3,750 ***
4,300		1-09	Capitol Odors	4,300	
129,695	75,000	1-09-04	Totals forward to next page	129,695	78,750

*Cash credit is to Miscellaneous Income, account #950.

**Cash credit is to Big City National Bank, account #101.

***Cash credit is to Income from Investments, account #920.

EXHIBIT 4
CASH DISBURSEMENTS JOURNAL
(selected portion)

Apple Blossom Cologne Company Cash Disbursements					Page 98
			DEBIT	CASH CREDIT	
	CHECK		ACCOUNT	BIG CITY	SECOND
DATE	NUMBER	PAYEE	NUMBER	NATL	NATL
12-23-03		Totals brought forward		212,000	113,511
12-24	1443	Alex McBane	301	650	
12-24	1444	United Fund	832	50	
12-24	1445	Office Decorators	301	350	
12-24	1446	Longhorn Garbage Disp.	301	135	
12-26	6889	Bert Campo	303		432
12-26	6890	Karl Marker	303		402
12-26	6891	Earnest Jones	303		470
12-26	6892	Patricia Sanders	303		402
12-26	6893	Bruce Jones	303		484
12-26	6894	Robert Smith	303		406
12-26	6895	Milton Schaefer	303		406
12-26	6896	Antonio Salvadore	303		468
12-26	6897	Susan Billingsley	303		468
12-26	6898	Robin Botner	303		486
12-26	6899	Raymond Arthur	303		460
12-26	6900	Bill Potet	303		428
12-26	6901	David Johnson	303		430
12-26	6902	Elizabeth Roberts	303		410
12-27	1447	Gulf States Oil Supply	830	345	
12-27	1448	Madison Advertising	301	1,225	
12-27	1449	DeBella Hardware	301	821	
12-30	1450	Quick Print Printers	301	744	
12-30	1451	Second National Bank	(See cash receipts journal)		
12-31	1452	Second National Bank	(See cash receipts journal)		
12-31-03		December totals		216,320	119,663
1-02-04	1453	Second National Bank	(See cash receipts journal)		
1-02	6903 -26	Salaried employees December			
		payroll	303		95,291
1-02	6927-40	Hourly employees, weekly			
		payroll	303		6,140
1-05	1454	Central Power & Light Co.	301	1,100	
1-05	1455	William F. Reimann	301	468	
1-06	1456	Hart Murphy Office Outfitters	301	8,400	
1-06	1457	Fulton Paper Co.	301	620	
1-07	1458	Hoffmann Supply Co.	301	240	
1-08	1459	A to Z Janitorial	301	230	
1-08	1460	Norton Exterminators	301	70	
1-08	1461	Fruit Juicy Perfume Co	301	109,120	
1-09	1462	Edwards, Overstreet, & Gilley	301	4,820	
1-09	1463	Flash Freight Co.	301	400	
1-09	1464	Apple Valley Security	301	1,485	
1-09	6941-54	Hourly employees, weekly			
		payroll	303		6,152
1-09	1465	Fruit Scents, Inc.	301	11,080	
1-09	1466	Dr. Edward Abel	301	50	
1-09-04		Totals carried forward		138,083	107,583

Apple Blossom Cologne Company — A-1

Bank Reconciliation - Big City National Bank

December 31, 2003

(Prepared by Client)

Balance Per Bank Statement				816660
Add:				
Deposit in transit		Dec. 29	45987	
Undeposited cash receipts		Dec. 31	12594	
				58581
Deduct: Checks outstanding				
No.	Payee			
1443	Alex McBane Heating	Dec. 24	650	
1445	Office Decorators	Dec. 24	350	
1446	Longhorn Garbage Disposal	Dec. 24	135	
1449	DeBella Hardware	Dec. 27	821	
1450	Quick Print Printers	Dec. 30	744	
1452	Second National Bank	Dec. 31	26000	28700
	Balance 12-31-03			846541

A-2

STANDARD FORM TO CONFIRM ACCOUNT BALANCE INFORMATION WITH FINANCIAL INSTITUTIONS

ORIGINAL

Apple Blossom Cologne Company
CUSTOMER NAME

Financial Institution's Name and Address

[Big City National Bank
Main at Michigan Avenue
Chicago, Illinois 60612]

We have provided to our accountants the following information as of the close of business on December 31, 2003, regarding our deposit and loan balances. Please confirm the accuracy of the information, noting any exceptions to the information provided. If the balances have been left blank, please complete this form by furnishing the balance in the appropriate space below.* Although we do not request nor expect you to conduct a comprehensive, detailed search of your records, if during the process of completing this confirmation additional information about other deposit and loan accounts we may have with you comes to your attention, please include such information below. Please use the enclosed envelope to return the form directly to our accountants.

1. At the close of business on the date listed above, our records indicated the following deposit balance(s):

ACCOUNT NAME	ACCOUNT NO.	INTEREST RATE	BALANCE*
Apple Blossom Cologne Company General Account	146-2013	N/A	$816,660

2. We were directly liable to the financial institution for loans at the close of business on the date listed above as follows:

ACCOUNT NO./ DESCRIPTION	BALANCE*	DATE DUE	INTEREST RATE	DATE THROUGH WHICH INTEREST IS PAID	DESCRIPTION OF COLLATERAL

Lillian Stockton
(Customer's Authorized Signature)

January 2, 2004
(Date)

The information presented above by the customer is in agreement with our records. Although we have not conducted a comprehensive, detailed search of our records, no other deposit or loan accounts have come to our attention except as noted below.

Buford Churchill
(Financial Institution Authorized Signature)

January 7, 2004
(Date)

Cashier
(Title)

EXCEPTIONS AND/OR COMMENTS

Please return this form directly to our accountants:

[Anderson, Olds, and Watershed
Certified Public Accountants
615 Big City Bank Building
Chicago, Illinois 60612]

* Ordinarily, balances are intentionally left blank if they are not available at the time the form is prepared.

Approved 1990 by American Bankers Association, American Institute of Certified Public Accountants, and Bank Administration Institute. Additional forms available from: AICPA—Order Department, P.O. Box 2209, Jersey City, NJ 07303-2209

D451 5951

Apple Blossom Cologne Company A-3

Bank Reconciliation - Second National Bank

December 31, 2003

(Prepared by Client)

Balance Per Bank Statement				2812
Add deposits in transit:				
		Dec. 30	10000	
		Dec. 31	26000	
				36000
Deduct: Checks outstanding				
No.	Payee			
6889	Bert Campo	Dec. 26	432	
6893	Bruce Jones	Dec. 26	484	
6897	Susan Billingsley	Dec. 26	468	
6899	Raymond Arthur	Dec. 26	460	1844
				36968

A-4

STANDARD FORM TO CONFIRM ACCOUNT BALANCE INFORMATION WITH FINANCIAL INSTITUTIONS

ORIGINAL

Apple Blossom Cologne Company
CUSTOMER NAME

We have provided to our accountants the following information as of the close of business on December 31, 2003, regarding our deposit and loan balances. Please confirm the accuracy of the information, noting any exceptions to the information provided. If the balances have been left blank, please complete this form by furnishing the balance in the appropriate space below.* Although we do not request nor expect you to conduct a comprehensive, detailed search of your records, if during the process of completing this confirmation additional information about other deposit and loan accounts we may have with you comes to your attention, please include such information below. Please use the enclosed envelope to return the form directly to our accountants.

Financial Institution's Name and Address
[Second National Bank
615 Lakeway Road
Chicago, Illinois 60614]

1. At the close of business on the date listed above, our records indicated the following deposit balance(s):

ACCOUNT NAME	ACCOUNT NO.	INTEREST RATE	BALANCE*
Apple Blossom Cologne Company Payroll Account	36-118-402	N/A	$2,812

2. We were directly liable to the financial institution for loans at the close of business on the date listed above as follows:

ACCOUNT NO./ DESCRIPTION	BALANCE*	DATE DUE	INTEREST RATE	DATE THROUGH WHICH INTEREST IS PAID	DESCRIPTION OF COLLATERAL

Lillian Stockton
(Customer's Authorized Signature)

January 2, 2004
(Date)

The information presented above by the customer is in agreement with our records. Although we have not conducted a comprehensive, detailed search of our records, no other deposit or loan accounts have come to our attention except as noted below.

Wesley Hart
(Financial Institution Authorized Signature)

January 6, 2004
(Date)

Cashier
(Title)

EXCEPTIONS AND/OR COMMENTS

Please return this form directly to our accountants:
[Anderson, Olds, and Watershed
Certified Public Accountants
615 Big City Bank Building
Chicago, Illinois 60612]

* Ordinarily, balances are intentionally left blank if they are not available at the time the form is prepared.

Approved 1990 by American Bankers Association, American Institute of Certified Public Accountants, and Bank Administration Institute. Additional forms available from: AICPA–Order Department, P.O. Box 2209, Jersey City, NJ 07303-2209

D451 5951

Apple Blossom Cologne Company A-6

Undeposited Cash Receipts - Big City National Bank

12-31-03

Payor		Date	Amount
Capitol Odors		12-30	2148
Janis Department Store		12-30	2000
Body Bar		12-30	2412
Lone Star Supply		12-30	1602
William's Fragrances		12-31	3618
National Gas		12-31	814
	Total		12594

The above checks were examined in my presence and returned to me intact on this date, 12-31-03, 3:45pm.

Pam Lewis
Cashier

Apple Blossom Cologne Company A-7

Petty Cash

12-31-03

Denomination		Number	Amount		Total
Currency		20	3	60	
		10	9	90	
		5	22	110	
		1	18	18	278
Coins		Halves	2	1	
		Quarters	40	10	
		Dimes	20	2	
		Nickels	80	4	
		Pennies	100	1	18
Checks			none	0	0
Total cash					296
Petty Cash Vouchers					
(1) Barker Office Supply			Dec. 28	82	
(2) U.S. Post Office- Stamps			Dec. 30	55	
(3) Bertram Hardware			Dec. 31	67	204
Balance 12/31/03					500

The above fund was examined in my presence and returned to me intact on this date, 12-31-03, 4:30pm.

Pam Lewis
Cashier

Assignment #4
Inventory and Purchases

The information that follows is grouped into two categories: (1) Internal Control and (2) Substantive Audit Procedures. This information is to be used to complete the exercises for this assignment. Do the *optional exercises* only if told to do so by your instructor.

RELEVANT INFORMATION

Internal Control

The Apple Blossom Cologne Company charges the net cost (including related freight, taxes, and discounts) of inventory purchases directly to the Inventory account. The company keeps a perpetual inventory record. At each year-end, a physical inventory is taken in order to adjust the ~~Cost of Goods Sold account to the~~ physical count. Any differences between the physical count and the perpetual records are charged or credited to Cost of Goods Sold.

Apple Blossom purchases the bulk of its inventory from two sources: Fruit Scents, Inc., in Hope, Michigan, and Fruit Juicy Perfume Company in Springfield, Missouri. All inventory is purchased by the case with each case holding 24 units (bottles, jars, or cans). All inventory received from vendors is stored in the warehouse until needed.

A voucher system is used for purchases. Vouchers are prepared when invoices are received and held in an unpaid voucher file (filed by payment date) until the cash disbursement is made. A voucher number is a two-number code with the first number representing the month in which the voucher was recorded and the second number representing the order in which the voucher was recorded during the month. For example, 10-7 would be the number for the seventh invoice recorded during the month of October.

Apple Blossom Cologne Company is a wholesale distributor. Products received from factory vendors are repackaged and distributed to retailers. Orders are processed as received from customers. As soon as an order is completed, it is shipped immediately. Timeliness is important because the company has very little room to store repackaged merchandise.

The following internal control questionnaire was completed for you by Jasper Parsons. Review this questionnaire and the permanent file material describing the control environment, and accounting and control procedures related to the Inventory-Purchases system. Your firm has found that personnel involved in this area are generally competent.

The Inventory-Purchases system initiates a cycle that begins with the requisition and purchase of materials and then proceeds to the recording of the liability for the purchase. You will study the recording of the liability for purchases in Assignment #8, which deals with accounts payable processing. As you read through the inventory and purchases material and analyze the questionnaire, keep in mind the six categories of control procedures: (1) segregation of duties, (2) access, (3) authorization, (4) input controls, (5) processing controls, and (6) output controls, as well as potential errors or irregularities.

Typical errors or irregularities in the inventory and purchases area include:

1 Inventory may have been shipped but not recorded.
2. Inventory usage may not have been accurately recorded.

3. Purchases may have been recorded but the merchandise not received.
4. Merchandise may have been received but not recorded in purchases.
5. Purchases may have been recorded erroneously.
6. Unauthorized purchases may have been made.
7. Inventory may have been stolen.
8. Inventory may have been improperly counted.
9. Inventory may have been improperly valued.

Internal Control Questionnaire–Inventory-Purchases System

	Yes	*No*	*Comments*
1. Is a physical inventory taken at least annually?	√	—	
2. Does the company prepare written instructions for inventory counts?	√	—	
3. Are such instructions followed by those taking the physical count?	√	—	
4. Are the inventory counts taken by personnel who are independent of the custody or recording of inventory?	—	√	Anita Columbo, the inventory clerk, helps count inventory
5. Are the inventories adequately safeguarded and controlled?	√	—	
6. Is a receiving report prepared for all receipts of merchandise?	√	—	
7. Is the purchasing function independent of receiving and accounting?	—	√	Receiving and purchasing are in the same department
8. Are purchases requisitions used?	√	—	
9. Are prenumbered purchase orders used?	√	—	
10. Are purchases authorized by responsible officials?	√	—	Mr. Brown signs the purchase orders.
11. Are all receipts properly counted and inspected?	√	—	
12. Does the company maintain a perpetual inventory system?	√	—	

	Yes	No	
13. Are such records maintained by someone who does not have custody of inventory?	—	√	Anita Columbo also maintains the inventory master records
14. Are discrepancies between the physical count and the perpetual records investigated periodically?	√	–	The controller maintains tight control over inventory discrepancies.

Substantive Audit Procedures–Inventory Balances

On January 1, when the client took the physical inventory, you were on hand to observe the count. Since the plant was shut down for the inventory taking on January 1, 2003, all finished goods were shipped prior to the shutdown. You may assume that there are no shipping cut-off problems. To facilitate the counting of inventory in the warehouse, the client moved some of it out onto the shipping dock. Both inventory areas were neat and orderly. You satisfied yourself that the client was using good control procedures. During your conversations with various client personnel you also formed the opinion that the inventory personnel were reasonably competent. When the inventory was completed, you obtained all count sheets from the client and summarized them on a working paper. This was done in order to allow you to agree the total count with the final priced inventory. This work sheet summarizing all the count sheets is presented as schedule C-2. As you observed the inventory, you recorded several test counts. These test counts are noted on schedule C-2 by a tick mark (n). You should prepare an inventory observation memorandum describing the work you did and any problems encountered or observed during the entire inventory process. (A form for that memorandum is referenced C-3.)

Don McKenna has compiled the final inventory, pricing it on a FIFO basis. He has provided you with a copy of that inventory and it is presented in the working papers as schedule C-1. You may assume that you have checked current replacement costs on all the inventory items and found that each exceeds its inventory carrying value.

You also asked Don McKenna to pull from the files the cash vouchers (along with supporting materials) for all inventory recorded as purchases by the Company for the current year. He did so and all the information from those vouchers has been summarized for you in Exhibit 5. (Exhibit 5 is being presented to you in lieu of the actual documents; as such, consider the material to represent the actual client documents belonging to the client and not the auditor.) You may assume that all vouchers have the appropriate supporting materials attached, that all vouchers have been properly approved, and that all information on the vendor's invoices is accurate. Use this information to perform the appropriate audit procedures.

Exercises

PART A–Control Risk Analysis (Optional Exercises)

1. Having reviewed the internal control questionnaire, as well as the Permanent File material describing the Inventory-Purchases system, prepare an internal control flowchart of Apple Blossom's Inventory-Purchases system. Use form P-6 (or software); the headings for the flowchart have been provided for you on this form. Show the flow of documentation, the steps involved in the process, and note any internal control features.

2. Describe the strengths (control procedures) related to Inventory-Purchases. For each strength, describe a test of controls that you could perform to test the operating effectiveness of the control. Use form CSF-4. Classify the strengths according to the six categories of control procedures (see General Instructions and Preparations).

3. For each weakness, list the weakness, a potential error or irregularity, as well as a compensating substantive test of transactions or balances to detect the error or irregularity, assuming the necessary records and documents are available to you. Use form CWF-4. Classify the weaknesses according to the six control procedure categories. You should keep these weaknesses in mind as you write the substantive audit steps in your programs.

4. Prepare a system audit program for the Inventory-Purchases system consisting of (1) tests of control to test internal control strengths (procedures); (2) substantive tests of transactions; and/or (3) dual-purpose tests, having both test of controls and substantive aspects. Utilize the analysis of strengths and weaknesses you have prepared to guide you, keeping internal control objectives and the financial statement assertions in mind as you prepare your program. Write your system audit program on form SP-4. Use the headings: Tests of Controls, Dual-Purpose Tests, and Substantive Tests of Transactions.

Part B–Assessing Audit Risk (Optional Exercises)

Before working the risk assessment exercises that follow, review the section entitled, Assessing Audit Risk, in the *General Instructions and Preparations* section of the case. To use the audit risk model for estimating the nature, extent, and timing of evidence, the auditor must first establish an acceptable overall audit risk (AR), then assess inherent risk (IR) and control risk (CR) for each assertion. The five financial statement assertions are (1) existence or occurrence, (2) completeness, (3) rights and obligations, (4) valuation or allocation, and (5) presentation and disclosure. Inherent risk is the probability that a misstatement occurs in an assertion. The more complex or subjective the account or class of transactions, the greater the inherent risk. The auditor assesses inherent risk by evaluating complexity, subjectivity, and related factors that may impact the risk of misstatements occurring in the account or class of transactions. The auditor assesses control risk by evaluating the effectiveness of controls in preventing or detecting material misstatements related to the assertion. After obtaining an understanding of internal control, the auditor determines an "assessed level of control risk." For a particular assertion, the assessed level may be 1.0 (100%), meaning the controls related to that assertion are nonexistent or not effective. If the auditor is able to identify controls that appear to be effective in preventing or detecting misstatements, the auditor may assess control risk at a level less than 1.0. If the assessed level is less than 1.0, the auditor has to support this assessment by performing tests of controls to determine whether the controls are effectively designed and are operating properly.

1. You have decided to assess the inherent risk associated with the assertion regarding the existence of inventory, specifically the assertion that "inventories included in the balance sheet physically exist." The Anderson, Olds, and Watershed audit manual sets out inherent risk assessments for various accounts and classes of transactions that you are able to use as a guide for setting inherent risk. The risk assessments in the audit manual use the following qualitative levels: *low, moderate, high,* and *maximum*. A low assessment corresponds to a .25 probability, moderate to .50, high to .75 and maximum to 1.0. The audit manual states that inherent risk associated with inventory assertions should normally not be designated at less than a "moderate" level. Write a memorandum for the file indicating what characteristics of inventory would indicate that an assessment of inherent risk at less than moderate is usually not warranted. Also state your assessment of inherent risk for the existence assertion.

2. Examine the internal control questionnaire for the Inventory-Purchases system. Identify those controls that directly relate to the assertion that inventories in the balance sheet physically exist. For each control identified, describe a misstatement that could occur if the control is not effective.

3. Assess the control risk with regard to the assertion that inventories included in the balance sheet physically exist, that is, assess how likely it would be that a material misstatement was not prevented or detected by the controls present in the Apple Blossom Cologne Company. Assess the control risk as low, moderate, high, or maximum.

4. Anderson, Olds, and Watershed would like to keep the overall audit risk (AR) at .03. Based on the inherent risk assessment in Exercise (1) above, your control risk assessment in Exercise (3) above, and an overall audit risk (AR) of .03, compute the detection risk. Associate the probabilities outlined in Exercise (1) with the qualitative risk levels you selected for inherent risk and control risk. On the basis of your calculation of detection risk, describe in a memorandum the timing and extent of your substantive testing related to the existence of inventory. In your memorandum, explain the specific audit tests you would conduct to verify existence. For each test, specify the timing of the test (interim or year-end) and designate the extent of testing. Use the following designations for the extent of testing: *minimum, moderate, extensive*. Explain why you chose that level of testing.

PART C–Dollar-Unit Variables Sampling (Optional Exercise)

You have decided to conduct a substantive test to determine whether recorded purchases are overstated. You will use dollar-unit (PPS) sampling for this test. The purchase vouchers that have been recorded by the client during the year are listed in Exhibit 5. The total of these vouchers is $1,588,384 (including the vouchers for freight). You have decided that for purposes of this test, your tolerable error should be $80,000. You expect a misstatement in the population of $16,000 based on experience with similar clients. The Anderson, Olds, and Watershed audit manual states that the acceptable risk of incorrect acceptance (ARIA) should be set at .05.

You will be selecting your sample from the population of the 1,588,384 dollars comprising purchases. The logical units that the dollars "hook" into are the twelve vouchers listed in Exhibit 5. The sample size is calculated as follows:

$$\text{Sample size} = \frac{\text{Population book value} \times \text{Reliability factor}}{\text{Tolerable misstatement} - (\text{Expected misstatement} \times \text{Expansion factor})}$$

Required:
1. State the objective of the test.
2. Define the population and the sampling unit.
3. Determine the appropriate sample size using the formula given above and the tables provided at the end of this assignment (round *up* to the nearest whole number). Calculate the sampling interval. Assume that misstated items are in error by the full dollar amount of the recorded value (100% misstatement).
4. Select the dollars to be included in your sample and determine the logical units (vouchers) to be selected for audit using systematic selection. (Be sure to use the total amount for each voucher as indicated by the double underlining. Also be sure to include the vouchers for freight.) Use a random start of 13,732. Spreadsheet software facilitates the calculations.
5. Assume that you perform auditing procedures (consisting of the examination of documents supporting the vouchers) on the vouchers associated with the dollars selected. The following information about the errors in the population of vouchers would not be known by the auditor. Nevertheless, you should use this information to determine which of the vouchers in your sample contain errors:

For purposes of this exercise only, assume that the logical units (vouchers) in the population contain the following errors:

Voucher No.	Recorded Amount	Correct Amount
5-21	$119,920	$109,920
12-35	11,080	5,080

None of the other ten vouchers contains an error.

6. Evaluate the results by determining the error bound for overstatements.
7. State your conclusion regarding the recorded balance of purchases. Use the Dollar Unit Sampling tables in this assignment to calculate the upper error bound. What action would you suggest the auditors should take at this point? (Note: *do not* prepare an adjustment for errors discovered.)

   (Note: to determine the upper error bound, consult the AICPA Auditing Practice Release, *Audit Sampling*, pp. 61-77, AICPA, 1999).

PART D–Required Exercises: Substantive Procedures

1. Prepare a substantive audit program for inventory balances. The construction of an audit program for inventory balances should begin with an explicit recognition of the five financial statement assertions. As you write your program, keep these assertions in mind: (1) existence or occurrence, (2) completeness, (3) rights and obligations, (4) valuation or allocation, and (5) presentation and disclosure. From these assertions, you should derive your specific audit objectives related to inventory balances.

   Your audit program should address the five financial statement assertions, as well as any weaknesses you have discovered in the control structure. In this regard, keep in mind the six categories of internal control. You may assume that you have satisfied yourself with respect to any assertions not specifically mentioned in the narrative.

   As you write your program, remember the generalized evidence-gathering procedures of (1) recalculation, (2) physical observation, (3) confirmation, (4) verbal inquiry, (5) vouching of documents, (6) tracing, (7) scanning, and (8) analytical procedures. Use them to help you write the specific evidence-gathering procedures in your program.

   Write your program on form AP-3. Use the financial statement assertions as your major headings.

2. Study the prior year's working papers C-1 to C-3. Then perform all required audit work on schedules C-1 and C-2 and write your inventory observation memorandum; reference the memorandum C-3.

P-6

APPLE BLOSSOM COLOGNE COMPANY

Inventory-Purchases System

Purchasing Agent	Inventory Clerk	Receiving

APPLE BLOSSOM COLOGNE COMPANY CSF-4

Inventory-Purchases System
Internal Control Strengths

<u>Strength</u>	<u>Possible Test of Controls</u>

APPLE BLOSSOM COLOGNE COMPANY CWF-4

Inventory-Purchases System
Internal Control Weaknesses

Weakness	Potential Error	Compensating Substantive Procedure

Inventory-Purchases
System Program

DOLLAR UNIT SAMPLING TABLES

Reliability Factors for Misstatements of Overstatement

Number of Overstatement Misstatements	*Risk of Incorrect Acceptance*								
	1%	*5%*	*10%*	*15%*	*20%*	*25%*	*30%*	*37%*	*50%*
0	4.61	3.00	2.31	1.90	1.61	1.39	1.21	1.00	.70
1	6.64	4.75	3.89	3.38	3.00	2.70	2.44	2.14	1.68
2	8.41	6.30	5.33	4.72	4.28	3.93	3.62	3.25	2.68
3	10.05	7.76	6.69	6.02	5.52	5.11	4.77	4.34	3.68
4	11.61	9.16	8.00	7.27	6.73	6.28	5.90	5.43	4.68
5	13.11	10.52	9.28	8.50	7.91	7.43	7.01	6.49	5.68
6	14.57	11.85	10.54	9.71	9.08	8.56	8.12	7.56	6.67
7	16.00	13.15	11.78	10.90	10.24	9.69	9.21	8.63	7.67
8	17.41	14.44	13.00	12.08	11.38	10.81	10.31	9.68	8.67
9	18.79	15.71	14.21	13.25	12.52	11.92	11.39	10.74	9.67
10	20.15	16.97	15.41	14.42	13.66	13.02	12.47	11.79	10.67
11	21.49	18.21	16.60	15.57	14.78	14.13	13.55	12.84	11.67
12	22.83	19.45	17.79	16.72	15.90	15.22	14.63	13.89	12.67
13	24.14	20.67	18.96	17.86	17.02	16.32	15.70	14.93	13.67
14	25.45	21.89	20.13	19.00	18.13	17.40	16.77	15.97	14.67
15	26.75	23.10	21.30	20.13	19.24	18.49	17.84	17.02	15.67
16	28.03	24.31	22.46	21.26	20.34	19.58	18.90	18.06	16.67
17	29.31	25.50	23.61	22.39	21.44	20.66	19.97	19.10	17.67
18	30.59	26.70	24.76	23.51	22.54	21.74	21.03	20.14	18.67
19	31.85	27.88	25.91	24.63	23.64	22.81	22.09	21.18	19.67
20	33.11	29.07	27.05	25.74	24.73	23.89	23.15	22.22	20.67

Expansion Factors for Expected Misstatements

Risk of Incorrect Acceptance %	*Factor*
1	1.90
5	1.60
10	1.50
15	1.40
20	1.30
25	1.25
30	1.20
37	1.15
50	1.10

Audit Program–Inventory Balances AP-3

Assertions

Begin with the list of assertions below and add others you think appropriate. Then write your audit program to test those assertions.

1. Inventory physically exists.
2. Inventory is owned by the company.
3. Inventory cost properly includes freight, discounts, taxes, etc.
4. Obsolete and unsalable goods have been written off or written down.
5. The inventory value does not exceed the applicable measure of market value.
6. Inventory out on consignment is properly recorded.
7. Inventory is a current asset.
8. Inventory pledged as collateral is disclosed.

Program Steps

Exhibit 5

Apple Blossom Cologne Company

Cash Vouchers

(with supporting materials attached)

2003 Vo. No.	Vendor	Item	Quantity (Cases)	Discount	Freight	Cost Per Case	Vendor's Invoice Date	Receiving Report Date	Date Paid	Amount Paid
1-24	Fruit Scents, Inc	#A601- Lemon Oil	600	Net 30	FOB Hope	120.80	1-23-03	1-24-03	2-11-03	72480
	Hope, Michigan	#A603- Lemon Oil	400	|	|	245.90	|	|	|	98360
		#A608- Lemon Oil	400	|	|	370.40	|	|	|	148160
		#L818- Smoothing Lotion	1200	|	|	72.80	|	|	|	87360
										406360
1-29	Flash Freight Co.	Freight on shipment paid by voucher #1-24 ($4.00 per case)	2600	cash	FOB Hope	4.00	1-28-00		2-17-00	10400
3-09	Fruit Juicy Perfume Co.	#L940- Skin Tone Lotion	500	Net 30	FOB Chi	86.40	3-4-03	3-10-03	2-26-03	43200
	Springfield, Missouri	#L612- Moisturizing Lotion	200	|	|	86.40	|	|	|	17280
		#L818 Smoothing Lotion	200	|	|	76.80	|	|	|	15360
										75840
5-21	Fruit Juicy Perfume Co.	#H84- 4 oz. Hand Creme	580	Net 30	FOB Chi	100.00	5-6-03	5-9-03	5-14-03	58000
	Springfield, Missouri	#F60- 4 oz. Face Creme	600	|	|	103.20	|	|	|	61920
										119920
6-34	Fruit Scents, Inc	#E807- L'Eau de Rose	200	Net 30	FOB Hope	552.80	6-25-03	6-26-03	7-1-03	110560
	Hope, Michigan	#R315- 4 oz. Apple Oil	400	|	|	216.80	|	|	|	86720
		#R320- 6 oz. Apple Oil	200	|	|	334.40	|	|	|	66880
		#Q291- 8 oz. Magnolia Oil	100	|	|	418.40	|	|	|	41840
										306000

Exhibit 5

Apple Blossom Cologne Company

Cash Vouchers

(with supporting materials attached)

2003 Vo. No.	Vendor	Item	Quantity (Cases)	Discount	Freight	Cost Per Case	Vendor's Invoice Date	Receiving Report Date	Date Paid	Amount Paid
7-11	Flash Freight Co.	Frieght on shipment paid by	900	cash	FOB Hope	4.00	7-11-03		7-21-03	3600
		voucher #6-34 (4.00 per case)								
9-14	Fruit Scents, Inc	#E801- L'Eau de Pomme	200	Net 30	FOB Hope	552.80	9-4-03	9-11-03	9-17-03	110560
	Hope, Michigan	#E802- L'Eau de Abricot	100	|	|	552.80	|	|	|	55280
		#E803- L'Eau de Teint	100	|	|	552.80	|	|	|	55280
		#E806- L'Eau de Citron	160	|	|	552.80	|	|	|	88448
		#E804- L'Eau de Chevrefeuille	100	|	|	552.80	|	|	|	55280
		#E805- L'Eau de Jasmine	80	|	|	552.80	|	|	|	44224
										409072
9-20	Fruit Scents, Inc	#E803- L'Eau de Teint	120	Net 30	FOB Hope	552.80	9-5-03	9-12-03	9-22-03	66336
	Hope, Michigan	#E806- L'Eau de Citron	120	|	|	552.80	|	|	|	66336
										132672
9-25	Flash Freight Co.	Freight on shipment paid by	980	cash	FOB Hope	4.00	9-15-03		9-22-03	3920
		voucher #9-14 and #9-25 ($4.00/case)								

Exhibit 5

Apple Blossom Cologne Company

Cash Vouchers

(with supporting materials attached)

2003 Vo. No.	Vendor	Item	Quantity (Cases)	Discount	Freight	Cost Per Case	Vendor's Invoice Date	Receiving Report Date	Date Paid	Amount Paid
12-21	Fruit Juicy Perfume Co.	#L940- Skin Tone Lotion	800	Net 30	FOB Chi	86.40	12-24-03	12-29-03	1-8-04	69120
	Springfield, Missouri	#H84- 4 oz. Hand Creme	400	|	|	100.00	|	|	|	40000
										109120
12-35	Fruit Scents, Inc	#A601 Lemon Oil	100	Net 30	FOB Hope	110.80	12-29-03	12-30-03	1-9-04	11080
	Hope, Michigan									
12-42	Flash Freight Co.	Freight on shipment paid by voucher #12-35 ($4.00 per case)	100	cash	FOB Hope	4.00	12-29-03		1-9-04	400

Apple Blossom Cologne Company C-1

Inventory

12-31-03

(Prepared by Client)

	Item	Size Ounces	Number of Cases	Number of Bottles (24/Case)	Total Ounces	Cost per Unit	Amount Inventory	Totals
Oils								
	#A601 Lemon	2	321	7704	15408	2.60/oz<	40061	
	#A603 Lemon	4	156	3744	14976	2.60/oz<	38938	
	#A608 Lemon	6	138	3312	19872	2.60/oz<	51667	
	#R315 Apple	4	102	2448	9792	2.30/oz<	22522	
	#R320 Apple	6	20	480	2880	2.35/oz<	6768	
	#Q291 Magnolia	8	21.5	516	4128	2.20/oz<	9082	
	Total Oils:							169038
Cremes								
	#H84 Hand Creme	4	590	14160	---	4.17/btl<	59047	
	#F60 Face Creme	4	540.5	12972	---	4.30/btl<	55780	
	Total Cremes							114827
Lotions								
	#L612 Moisturizing	8	820	19680	---	3.60/btl<	70848	
	#L940 Skin Tone	8	615	14760	---	3.60/btl<	53136	
	#L818 Smoothing	8	105	2520	---	3.20/btl<	8064	
	Total Lotions							132048
Colognes								
	#E801 L'Eau de Pomme	8	120	2880	23040	2.90/oz<	66816	
	#E802 L'Eau de Abricot	8	54	1296	10368	2.90/oz<	30067	
	#E803 L'Eau de Teint	8	110	2640	21120	2.90/oz<	61248	
	#E804 L'Eau de Chevrefeuell	8	58	1392	11136	2.90/oz<	32294	
	#E805 L'Eau de Jasmin	8	45	1080	8640	2.90/oz<	25056	
	#E806 L'Eau de Citron	8	60	1440	11520	2.90/oz<	33408	
	#E807 L'Eau de Rose	8	98.5	2364	18912	2.90/oz<	54845	
	Total Colognes							303734
			3974.5	95388	------	------	------	719647

Apple Blossom Cologne Company — C–2

Inventory Observation and Test Counts

December 31, 2003

Stock Number	Item	Number of Cases	Number of Bottles (24/Case)	Size of Bottle	Total Ounces
STOREROOM:			C		
L940	Skin Tone Lotion	615n	14760	8 oz	118080
L612	Moisturizing Lotion	820n	19680	8 oz	157440
L818	Smoothing Lotion	105n	2520	8 oz	20160
E806	L' Eau de Citron Cologne	60	1440	8 oz	11520
E807	L' Eau de Rose Cologne	98.5	2364	8 oz	18912
E801	L' Eau de Pomme Cologne	120n	2880	8 oz	23040
E803	L' Eau de Teint Cologne	90	2160	8 oz	17280
E802	L' Eau d' Abricot Cologne	54	1296	8 oz	10368
F60	Face Crème**	430.5n	10332	4 oz	41328
H84	Hand Creme	510n	12240	4 oz	48960
A608	Lemon Oil	138n	3312	6 oz	19872
A603	Lemon Oil	156n	3744	4 oz	14976
A601	Lemon Oil	321n	7704	2 oz	15408
E804	L' Eau de Chevrefeuille	58n	1392	8 oz	11136
E805	L' Eau de Jasmin Cologne	45	1080	8 oz	8640
Q291	Magnolia Oil	21.5	516	8 oz	4128
R315	Apple Oil	102n	2448	4 oz	9792
R320	Apple Oil	20	480	6 oz	2880
	Storeroom Total	3765	90348		553920
SHIPPING DOCK:					
F60	Face Creme	110	2640	4 oz	10560
E803	L' Eau de Teint Cologne	20	480	8 oz	3840
H84	Hand Creme	80	1920	4 oz	7680
	Shipping Dock Total	210	5040		22080
	Total Inventory		95388		576000

C After testing 30 upopened cases, bottle count on vendor's label accepted on unopened cases.

n Test counted during observation. No errors oberved.

NOTE: No obsolete or damaged inventory was oberved.

** For cutoff last receiving report #12–12 was used on 12/31/03. 150 cases of #F60 Face Crème were received from Fruit Juicy Perfume Co. That shipment included in above inventory.

Apple Blossom Cologne Company
Inventory Observation Memo
December 31, 2003

C-3

Assignment #5
Prepaid Expenses

To begin your work in the prepaid expenses area, review the work done in the prior year's working papers, D-1 to D-3. The client has various types of prepaid expense accounts: insurance, rent, office supplies, and small tools.

Prepaid Insurance

Study schedule D-1 in the prior year's working papers. Particularly note the procedures performed, the system of "tick marks" used, and the system of cross-referencing.

The company had been carrying one and one-half million dollars of insurance coverage on its plant and inventory. Due to the expansion into new markets, however, the coverage was increased by $1,000,000. Liability coverage amounting to $500,000 is carried on the delivery trucks. The salespersons' automobiles are covered with liability, collision, and comprehensive. Some of the company's employees are covered by fidelity bonds.

You may assume that you were able to read all the insurance policies currently in force noting coverage, term, and premiums. You also examined the vouchers (3-03 and 6-02) for the payments made on the truck liability policy, number AB6048R4, and on the fire and extended coverage policy, number 4628-41-8002.

Apple Blossom Cologne Company carries all the insurance through one agency, the Pierce and Langdohl Agency. You requested and received a confirmation from that agency on all policies currently in force. That confirmation is included in the working papers as schedule D-2.

Prepaid Rent

Apple Blossom Cologne Company leases from United Properties, Inc. a small warehouse located only a short distance from the main plant. During 2003 the warehouse was empty and not used, but Apple Blossom wanted to have it available for future use. The lease agreement had a 10-year term (cancelable only for nonpayment of rent) and was executed on May 1, 2000. It provided for a two-year rental of $7,500 to be paid in advance on May 1 of each even numbered year beginning May 1, 2000. You may assume that your firm has examined the lease and vouched the details in a prior year audit.

Office Supplies and Small Tools

As Apple Blossom Cologne Company purchases office supplies and small tools, the bookkeeper debits directly the Office Supplies Inventory and Small Tools Inventory accounts, #112 and #113, respectively. A physical inventory of each item is taken at year-end to determine what balance should be reported on the balance sheet. This physical count also enables the company to determine what the expense of the period was for office supplies and small tools. You were present on January 1, 2004 to observe the taking of the office supplies and small tools inventory and found that the counts of office supplies and small tools inventories amounted to $9,964 and $6,541, respectively.

Required Exercises

1. Prepare a substantive audit program for prepaid expense transactions and balances.

   The construction of a program for prepaid expenses should begin with an explicit recognition of the five financial statement assertions: (1) existence or occurrence, (2) completeness, (3) rights and obligations, (4) valuation or allocation, and (5) presentation and disclosure. From these assertions, you should derive your specific audit objectives related to prepaid expense transactions and balances.

   Your audit program should address the five financial statement assertions, as well as any weaknesses in the system of internal control. In this regard, keep in mind the six categories of control procedures. You may assume that you have satisfied yourself with respect to any assertions not specifically mentioned in the narrative.

   Also remember the generalized evidence-gathering procedures of (1) recalculation, (2) physical observation, (3) confirmation, (4) verbal inquiry, (5) vouching of documents, (6) tracing. (7) scanning, and (8) analytical procedures. Use them to help you write the specific evidence-gathering procedures in the program.

   Use form AP-4 to write your program. Use the financial statement assertions as the major headings in your program.

2. Prepare a summary schedule of prepaid insurance and insurance expense similar to D-1 in the prior year's working papers. Also perform any required work on schedule D-2 and include it with your working papers.

   Study the analytical procedures performed on working paper D-3 included in the prior year's working papers. Prepare a similar working paper to analyze the Prepaid Rent, Office Supplies Inventory, and Small Tools Inventory accounts. In discussing fluctuations in these accounts with the client, you were satisfied with the explanations provided, i.e., that the fluctuations reflected proper changes in operating costs.

Substantive Audit Program–Prepaid Expenses

Assertions

Begin with the list of assertions below and add others you think appropriate. Then write your audit program to test those assertions.

1. Prepaid expenses are bona fide expenditures paid by the company.
2. All prepaid expenses have been recorded.
3. Prepaid expense balances represent a proper allocation between asset and expenses.
4. Prepaid expenses are proper deferrals.

Program Steps

D-2

Pierce and Langdohl Insurance Agency

5806 Brunt Road
Chicago, Illinois 60616
Phone 312-555-3804

January 15, 2004

Anderson, Olds and Watershed
Certified Public Accountants
615 Big City Bank Building
Chicago, Illinois 60612

This is to confirm that during 2003, Apple Blossom Cologne Company had the following insurance policies listed with this agency:

Southwestern Fire and Casualty: Policy #4628-41-8001, fire and extended coverage on plant building and contents, $1,500,000, dated July 1, 2001, 2-year term, premium $17,562. Policy #4628-41-8002, fire and extended coverage on plant building and contents, $2,500,000, dated July 1, 2003, 2-year term, premium $31,250.

Old Line Insurance Group: Policy # AB6048R3, truck liability, $500,000, dated March 31, 2002, 1-year term, premium $4,918. Policy #AB6048R4, Truck liability, $500,000, dated March 31, 2003, 1-year term, premium $4,815.

State Mutual: Policy #60-218049, public liability (50K-100K-10K), collision ($100 ded.), and comprehensive ($100 ded.), dated October 1, 2001, 3-year term, premiums $17,703--liability, $13,067--collision, and $7,587--comprehensive.

American Fidelity and Casualty: Policy #KH-8034, fidelity bond on employees, $250,000, dated June 30, 2002, 3-year term, premium $8,810.

Sincerely yours,

William J. Ruppersen, Agent
PIERCE AND LANGDOHL AGENCY

WIR/jap

Assignment #6
Investments in Securities

The information that follows is grouped into two categories: 1) Internal Control and 2) Substantive Audit Procedures. This information is to be used to complete the exercises for this assignment.

Relevant Information

Internal Control

From time to time, Apple Blossom Cologne Company invests excess funds in marketable securities and occasionally longer term investments. Since the company does not hold these securities to generate income on short-term price differences, the securities are considered to be "available for sale." The Company has decided to expand into the nonfluorocarbon aerosol market in 2004. Accordingly, Ms. Stockton has been investing in short term securities in anticipation of this expansion. These securities have been classified as current assets, since they will be used in current operations. Ms. Stockton maintains custody of all securities and investments, while the accounting department records the transactions.

The following internal control questionnaire was completed by Jasper Parsons before he left the firm. Review this questionnaire before you write your substantive audit program.

As you study the questionnaire, keep in mind the six categories of internal control: (1) segregation of duties, (2) access, (3) authorization, (4) input controls, (5) processing controls, and (6) output controls. Then try to determine the types of errors or irregularities that could occur.

Internal Control Questionnaire—Investments in Securities

	Yes	*No*	*Comments*
1. Is the custody of securities kept separate from the accounting for those securities?	√	_	Treasurer maintains custody; controller records transactions.
2. Are securities kept in a safety deposit box?	√	_	Accessible only to Mrs. Stockton.
3. Are individual purchases and sales of securities authorized by the board of directors?	_	√	General authorization given to Mrs. Stockton.
4. Does the accounting department maintain a record of all securities?	√	_	
5. Does the accounting department maintain an independent record of income from investments?	_	√	Receives listing from treasurer.
6. Are securities periodically counted by someone other than the custodian?	_	√	

Substantive Audit Procedures—Transactions and Balances

On December 31, 2003, you were accompanied by the treasurer, Lillian Stockton, to the Big City National Bank where you were allowed to examine all the securities currently held by Apple Blossom Cologne Company in the company's safety deposit box. You prepared a schedule documenting your examination. It is included in the working papers referenced E-2.

After returning to the plant you had Apple Blossom request a letter from its broker, Roberts and Underwood, confirming all securities transactions for the year. The confirmation is provided as schedule E-4. You also asked Don McKenna to print out the general ledger page for the Income from Investments account. This is provided for you as schedule E-5.

You may assume that you traced all proceeds from the sale of investments into the cash receipts journal and the broker's advice for each transaction. You may also assume that you traced gains and losses from the sale of securities to the general ledger. When you examined the Income from Investments account, you checked all dividend rates against the Standard and Poor's *Annual Dividend Records*. No exceptions were found. From *The Wall Street Journal*, dated January 2, 2004, you observed that the market prices of securities held by Apple Blossom Cologne Company were as follows:

	Market	
McCormick Milling	$51/share	
Omega Data Systems	75.50/share	
SolarEnergy.com	16/share	
Southwestern Telecom	88/share	
Sears Credit Corporation debentures	$71,625	(@ 95.5)

Required Exercises

1. Prepare a substantive audit program for investments in securities transactions and balances. The construction of a program for securities transactions and balances should begin with an explicit recognition of the five financial assertions: (1) existence or occurrence, (2) completeness, (3) rights and obligations, (4) valuation or allocation, and (5) presentation and disclosure. From these assertions, you should derive your specific audit objectives related to investment transactions and balances.

   Your audit program should address the five financial statement assertions, as well as any weaknesses in the control structure. Keep in mind the six categories of control procedures. You may assume that you have satisfied yourself with respect to any assertions not specifically mentioned in the narrative.

   As you write your program, remember the generalized evidence-gathering procedures of (1) recalculation, (2) physical observation, (3) confirmation, (4) verbal inquiry, (5) vouching of documents, (6) tracing, (7) scanning, and (8) analytical procedures. Use them to help you write the specific evidence-gathering procedures in your program.

   Write your program on form AP-5. Use the financial statement assertions as the major headings in your program and list the appropriate steps under each of these captions. Whenever a program step addresses a weakness, as indicated by a "no" answer on the internal control questionnaire, reference the appropriate question number, e.g., Q-1, Q-2, etc.

2. Study the prior year's working papers, referenced E-1 to E-4, as well as the current applicable Financial Accounting Standards Board pronouncements pertaining to investments in securities. Perform your audit work collecting evidence from the client-prepared schedules, minutes of the Board of Directors, this narrative, and whatever other sources you deem necessary. Prepare schedule E-1, similar to that found in the prior year's working papers, to analyze Apple Blossom's Investments in Securities account (#115). Also, show any required audit work on working paper E-2.

Prepare schedule E-3 to analyze the gain/loss on sale of marketable securities and perform your audit work on schedule and E-5 to audit income from securities. Also perform the required audit work on schedule E-4. Apple Blossom's *equity securities* are all considered "available for sale" and will be used in current operations. Consequently, these securities are classified as *current assets*.

On July 2, 2003, Ms. Stockton purchased an investment in the bonds of Sears Credit Corporation. These bonds are ten year debentures with an issue date of July 1, 1998, maturing on July 1, 2008, and bearing 10% interest payable on July 1 and January 1 of each year; the yield on these bonds is 11%. *Apple Blossom intends to hold these bonds until maturity.* After examining the applicable Financial Accounting Standards Board pronouncements, determine whether you need to prepare a schedule (reference E-6) to reflect the proper treatment of the investment in the debt securities. If necessary, prepare schedule E-6 to analyze any required transfers out of the current Investments in Securities account.

Audit Program–Investments in Securities AP-5

Assertions

Begin with the list of assertions below and add others you think appropriate. Then write your audit program to test those assertions.

1. Investment securities are on hand or are properly held by a trustee.
2. All investment income has been received and recorded.
3. Investment cost does not exceed market value.
4. Investments pledged as collateral are properly disclosed.

Program Steps

Apple Blossom Cologne Company E-2

Securities Examination

12-31-03

The following securities were examined at a safety deposit box at Big City National Bank registered in the name of Apple Blossom Cologne Co.

	Certificate Number		Number of Shares or Securities
Southwestern Telecom	21		1425
McCormick Milling	7114		200
SolarEnergy.com	618		600
Sears Credit Corp. bonds in $1,000 denominations; 10% due July 2009; issue date: July 1, 1999.	2341 – 2415		75

The above listed securities were examined in my presence and returned to me intact on December 31, 2003 at 11:30 am.

Lillian Stockton

Treasurer, Apple Blossom Cologne Company

E-4

ROBERTS AND UNDERWOOD

Securities Brokers

1218 Northern Expressway * Chicago, Illinois

Phone: 312-555-6901

January 9, 2004

Anderson, Olds and Watershed
Certified Public Accountants
615 Big City Bank Building
Chicago, Illinois 60612

As per the request of our client, Apple Blossom Cologne Company, we are providing this detail listing of the transactions we have executed for the account of Apple Blossom during the calendar year 2003.

Date	Bought (Sold)		Amount	Commission	Net
1/30	(1270 sh.)	Lackawanna Energy	$170,180	127	170,053
4/17	(1686 sh.)	United Grain @ $120.00	202,230	40	202,190
7/2	75	Ten year 10% debentures of Sears Credit Corp, $75,000 par to yield 11%	72,000	173	72,173
7/21	200 sh.	McCormick Wheat & Milling @ $48.00	9,600	50	9,650
8/19	600 sh.	SolarEnergy.com @ $21.50	12,900	60	12,960
12/29	500 sh.	Omega Data Systems @ $75.00	37,500	100	37,600

The Omega Data Systems securities have been purchased for Apple Blossom Cologne Company. The certificates are being held by this office pending payment by Apple Blossom.

ROBERTS AND UNDERWOOD
James Whitcomb
Account Manager

JAW/amr

E-5

Apple Blossom Cologne Company

General Ledger Report
Income from Investments
Account Number 920

Date	Item Description	Details: Shares	Details: Per Share Income	Debit	Credit	Balance
3/31	Dividends:					
	Southwestern Telecom	1,425	$0.60		855	855
	United Grain	1,686	$1.55		2,613	3,468
6/30	Dividends:					
	Southwestern Telecom	1,425	$0.60		855	4,323
9/30	Dividends:					
	Southwestern Telecom	1,425	$0.60		855	5,178
	McCormick Milling	200	$1.30		260	5,438
	SolarEnergy.com	600	$0.70		420	5,858
12/12	Dividends:					
	Southwestern Telecom	1,425	$0.60		855	6,713
	McCormick Milling	200	$1.30		260	6,973
	SolarEnergy.com	600	$0.70		420	7,393
	Year-end balance					7,393

Assignment #7
Property, Plant, and Equipment (Fixed Assets)

The information that follows is grouped into two categories: (1) Internal Control and (2) Substantive Audit Procedures. This information is to be used to complete the exercises.

Relevant Information

Internal Control

The following internal control questionnaire was completed by Jasper Parsons. Review this questionnaire before you write your substantive audit program. Keep in mind the six categories of control procedures: (1) segregation of functions, (2) access, (3) authorization, (4) input controls, (5) processing controls, and (6) output controls. Then try to determine potential errors that could occur.

Internal Control Questionnaire–Property, Plant, and Equipment

	Yes	*No*	*Comments*
1. Are purchases of fixed assets initiated by the purchasing agent?	√		
2. Are all purchases of fixed assets approved by the Board of Directors?	√		
3. Does the company have a policy for distinguishing between those items that are to be capitalized and those that are to be expensed as repairs and maintenance?		√	Except for items authorized by board, left to discretion of bookkeeper.
4. Are all retirements authorized by a responsible official?	√		Theodore Brown
5. Are there procedures in effect to assure that all retirements are recorded?	√		Retirement work orders are used.
6. Does the company maintain a fixed asset subsidiary ledger?	√		
7. Is the fixed asset subsidiary ledger reconciled to the control account periodically?	√		
8. Are periodic comparisons made between the fixed asset subsidiary ledger and the actual assets?	√		Every three years.

Substantive Audit Procedures

Before you begin your work on fixed assets, carefully study the prior year's working papers. For the current year, you had Don McKenna prepare two schedules, referenced F-2 and F-3, providing a detailed analysis of the additions and disposals to the fixed asset and accumulated depreciation accounts.

You also had Don prepare a computation of depreciation. This schedule is referenced F-4. Apple Blossom uses straight-line depreciation for all fixed assets. The useful life is 30 years on all buildings, 20 years on all machinery and equipment, four years on all automotive equipment, and 20 years on all furniture and fixtures. These useful lives were adopted by Apple Blossom after a joint session between their management and your audit firm several years ago. Also discussed in that meeting was the amount of depreciation to take in the year a fixed asset was acquired or disposed of. It was decided that, while it was more accurate to take depreciation for the exact number of months the assets were owned, it was more practical to take one-half year of depreciation in the year acquired and one-half year depreciation in the year of disposal. The firm has been following that policy.

With regard to additions to fixed assets, you may assume that on December 30, 2003, when you first visited the client's plant, you were given a guided tour of the facilities. You were able to move freely around the plant during the inventory observation on January 1, 2004. While walking around in the client's plant, you toured with "eyes open." After examining the additions to fixed assets schedule prepared by Don McKenna, you could recall having seen each of the fixed asset additions as you toured the client's facilities.

Don McKenna pulled from the files all cash vouchers and supporting materials for all disbursements related to fixed asset additions and repair and maintenance expense. Don summarized all the information from those vouchers in Exhibit 6. (This information is being provided to you in lieu of the actual client documents. Treat this material as though it were the actual client documents belonging to the client and not the auditor.) You may assume that all the vouchers have the appropriate supporting materials attached and that all vouchers have been approved.

With regard to the disposal of fixed assets, you may assume that the client maintains a detailed fixed asset subsidiary ledger from which you were able to obtain the cost and acquisition dates of assets retired or otherwise disposed of. You were able to agree the cost and acquisition dates of the disposal on schedule F-3 with the fixed asset subsidiary ledger. You may also assume that you traced the cash proceeds from the fixed asset disposal transaction into the cash receipts journal.

Equipment Lease

Apple Blossom entered into a lease contract on July 1, 2003, with Fizor Leasing Corporation to lease a Holtzmann spray bottle packaging machine. Fizor installed the machinery on July 1, 2003. You may assume that you read a copy of the lease, excerpts of which are as follows:

1. The lease is 10 years; noncancellable.
2. Payments will be made in ten equal annual installments of $12,701 beginning July 1, 2004.
3. The equipment has a fair market value of $74,800, an estimated life of 10 years, and no residual value.
4. Apple Blossom will pay all associated costs including insurance, maintenance, and property taxes.
5. The equipment reverts to Fizor at the termination of the lease.
6. Fizor expects a 11% return on its investment. This rate is the same as Apple Blossom's borrowing rate of 11%. The present value of the lease payments equals the fair market value of the equipment.

Assume that you have satisfied yourself as to the fair market value of the equipment at July 1, 2003.

Required Exercises

1. Prepare a substantive audit program for fixed asset transactions and balances.

   The construction of a program for fixed asset transactions and balances should begin with an explicit recognition of the five financial statement assertions: (1) existence or occurrence, (2) completeness, (3) rights and obligations, (4) valuation or allocation, and (5) presentation and disclosure. From these assertions, you should derive your specific audit objectives related to fixed asset transactions and balances.

   Your audit program should address the five financial statement assertions, as well as any weaknesses in the control structure. In this regard, keep in mind the six categories of control procedures. You may assume that you have satisfied yourself with respect to any assertions not specifically mentioned in the narrative.

   As you write your program, remember the generalized evidence-gathering procedures of (1) recalculation, (2) physical observation, (3) confirmation, (4) verbal inquiry, (5) vouching of documents, (6) tracing, (7) scanning, and (8) analytical procedures. Use them to help you write the specific evidence-gathering procedures in your program.

   Use form AP-6 to write your program. Use the financial statement assertions as the major headings in your program. List the appropriate audit steps under each of these captions.

2. Prepare a summary schedule of property, plant, and equipment similar to schedule F-1 in the prior year working papers. Also complete your audit work on schedules F-2, F-3, and F-4.

   A final schedule prepared for you in the fixed assets area by Don McKenna is an analysis of the Repairs and Maintenance account. This schedule is referenced F-5. Carefully examine the vouchers listed on this schedule and in Exhibit 6 to determine whether items were properly treated. Prepare any adjustments you believe are necessary.

3. After examining the proper Financial Accounting Standards Board pronouncements, determine whether you need to prepare a schedule (reference F-6, if necessary) to analyze the lease arrangement.

Substantive Audit Program–Property, Plant and Equipment

Assertions

Begin with the list of assertions below and add others you think appropriate. Then write your audit program to test those assertions.

1. All recorded fixed assets are in productive use.
2. All asset disposals have been recorded.
3. All asset additions have been recorded.
4. Repair and maintenance expenses have not been capitalized.
5. Asset additions have not been charged to repairs and maintenance expense.
6. All freight, installation, taxes, etc. on additions have been capitalized.
7. Depreciation has been calculated accurately.
8. Assets pledged as collateral have not been improperly removed.

Program Steps

Exhibit 6

Apple Blossom Cologne Company

Cash Vouchers for Property, Plant, and Equipment Disbursements--2003

(with supporting materials attached)

2003 Vo. No.	Vendor	Item	Discount	Terms Freight	Cost	Vendor's Invoice Date	Receiving Report Date	Date Paid	Amount Paid
2-18	Smith & Lewis Contractors Chicago, Illinois	Repair leaks in roof of warehouse	Cash	- - -	3190	2-4-03	- - -	2-4-03	3190
3-25	Stark Equipment Michigan City, Indiana	Repair parts for forklift tractors	Net 30	FOB Chi	1800	3-14-03	3-20-03	3-28-03	1800
5-40	Stark Equipment Michigan City, Indiana	Two Stark G720 forklift tractors	Net 30	FOB Chi	23200	5-16-03	5-21-03	5-26-03	23200
8-19	Simon-Weller Manu. Co. Gary, Indiana	Simon-Weller pneumatic packaging machine	Net 30	FOB Chi	210000	8-4-03	8-18-03	8-26-03	210000
8-21	Simon-Weller Manu. Co. Gary, Indiana	Installation of automated packaging assembly	Net 30	- - -	2650	8-8-03	- - -	8-26-03	2650
8-30	Myers Belt & Conveyor	Conveyor system for loading trucks on shipping dock	Net 30	FOB Chi	271600	8-1-03	8-6-03	8-29-00	2800
9-12	Kopel and Kopel Chicago, Illinois	Rearrange machinery for new conveyor system	Net 30	- - -	3600	9-2-03	- - -	9-24-03	3600
12-01	Alex McBane Heating & Air Conditioning	Annual servicing of furnace and heating system	Cash	- - -	650	12-23-03	- - -	12-23-03	650
12-10	Hart Murphy Office Outfitters Chicago, Illinois	One Zorex office photocopy machine	Net 30	FOB Chi	8400	12-10-03	12-10-03	1-7-04	8400

Apple Blossom Cologne Company F-2

Additions to Property, Plant, and Equipment

12-31-03

Vo. No.	Vendor	Item Description	Cost
	Stark Equipment	Two Stark G720 Forklift	23200
	Michigan City, IN	tractors @ $11,600 ea.	
8-19	Simon-Weller Manufactur-	One Simon-Weller	210000
	ing, Gary, IN	pneumatic packaging	
		machine	
8-30	Meyers Belts & Conveyors	Complete conveyor system	271600
	Chicago, IL	for loading trucks on	
		shipping dock	
12-10	Hart-Murphy Office	One Zorex office photocopy	8400
	Outfitters	machine	
	Chicago, IL		
			513200

Apple Blossom Cologne Company F-3

Retirements of Property, Plant, and Equipment

12-31-03

(Prepared by Client)

Journal Vo. No.	Asset Description		Date Acquired	Date Sold	Depreciation Rate-Method		Cost	Accum, Deprec.	Book Value	Proceeds	Gain (Loss) on Disposal
8-32	Machinery and equipment		5-20-97	8-20-03	5%	S. L.					
	3-ton heavy duty ceiling hoist						39600	11880	27720	12450	(15270)
							39600	11880	27720	12450	(15270)

Apple Blossom Cologne Company F-4

Depreciation Computation

12-31-03

(Prepared by client)

	Asset	Amount	Rate	2003 Deprec. Provision	Totals
	BUILDINGS:				
	Held full year	276263	3.33%	9209	
	Additions	---	---		
	Retirements	---	---		9209
	MACH. & EQUIPMENT:				
	Held full year	540845	5.00%	27042	
	Additions	513200	2.50%	12830	
	Retirements	39600	2.50%	990	40862
	AUTOMOTIVE:				
	Held full year	99425	25.00%	24856	
	Additions	---	---		
	Retirements	---	---		24856
	OFFICE FURN & FIXTURES:				
	Held full year	106433	5.00%	5322	
	Additions	8400	2.50%	210	
	Retirements	---	---		5532
				80459	80459

Apple Blossom Cologne Company — F-5

Repairs and Maintenance Account

12-31-03

(Prepared by client)

Vo. No.	Vendor	Item Description			Cost	
2-18	Thompson Industrial Chicago, IL	Repair parts for overhead retrieval system			3190	
3-25	Stark Equipment Michigan City, IN	Repairs to forklift tractor			1800	
8-21	Simon-Weller Manu Gary. IN	Installation of Simon-Weller packa machine			2650	X
9-12	Kapel and Kapel Barrington, IL	Rearrange machinery in plant for new conveyor system			3600	X
12-01	Alex McBane Heat. & Air Cond. Chicago, IL	Annual servicing of furnace & heating systems			650	
					11890	
		Vouchers less than $500 not listed			2350	
					14240	

Assignment #8
Accounts Payable Processing and Unrecorded Liabilities

The information that follows is grouped into two categories: 1) Internal Control and 2) Substantive Audit Procedures. This information is to be used to complete the exercises for this assignment. Do the optional exercises only if told to do so by your instructor.

Relevant Information

Internal Control

The Apple Blossom Cologne Company uses a voucher system to make cash disbursements and also maintains an accounts payable subsidiary ledger that provides a record of the total amount owed to each vendor. Vouchers are prepared as invoices are received and are held in an unpaid voucher file (filed by payment date) until the cash is disbursed. A voucher number is a two-number code with the first number representing the month in which the voucher was recorded and the second number representing the order in which the voucher was recorded in the month. For example, 11-3 would be the voucher number for the third invoice recorded in the month of November. The following internal control questionnaire was prepared for you by Jasper Parsons. Study the questionnaire in order to analyze Apple Blossom's control over accounts payable. Parker Shelton explained to you that Dave Dull, the accounts payable clerk, made occasional errors but was improving.

While going through the questionnaire, think about the six categories of control procedures: (1) segregation of functions, (2) access, (3) authorization, (4) input controls, (5) processing controls, and (6) output controls, and consider errors or irregularities that could occur. Also review the Permanent File narrative related to accounts payable.

Typical accounts payable errors or irregularities include:

1. Purchases may have been recorded in the wrong account.
2. A liability may have been recorded for a fictitious company.
3. The purchase and liability may have been recorded in the wrong accounting period.
4. A purchase or liability may have been omitted.
5. Purchases may have been recorded but the merchandise may not have been received.

Internal Control Questionnaire–Accounts Payable Processing

	Yes	*No*	*Comments*
1. Does the company maintain a voucher system?	√	_	
2. Are vouchers approved by a responsible official before payment?	√	_	Controller initials them.
3. Does a responsible official review the debit distribution of vouchers for proper recording?	_	√	Occasionally controller.

Question	Yes	No	Remarks
4. Are all purchases of merchandise and services recorded in the voucher register before disbursement?	_	√	Some invoices are run directly through cash disbursements application.
5. Does the company maintain an accounts payable subsidiary ledger?	√	_	
6. Is the accounts payable subsidiary ledger reconciled monthly with the accounts payable control account?	_	√	Balancing report is printed by software.
7. Are vendors' monthly statements reconciled to the accounts payable subsidiary ledger?	_	√	
8. Do adjustments to accounts payable require the approval of a responsible official?	√	_	Controller initials.
9. Are all vendors' invoices checked for proper pricing, extensions, footings, and terms?	_	√	Occasionally.
10. Does the company ensure that claims for damaged merchandise are processed promptly?	_	√	
11. Are unmatched invoices, receiving reports, and purchase orders reviewed periodically?	_	√	
12. Are supporting documents reviewed by check signers prior to payment?	√	_	
13. Are supporting documents stamped "cancelled" by the check signers?	√	_	Mrs. Stockton cancels them.
14. Are checks mailed directly by the person signing the check and not returned to preparers?	_	√	Mailed by accounts payable clerk.

Having reviewed the internal control questionnaire and the permanent file material, you should now be in a position to evaluate the internal control procedures.

Substantive Audit Procedures: Accounts Payable Balances

A schedule of accounts payable due as of December 31, 2003, was prepared by Dave Dull. The schedule is referenced G-1. You requested Dave to pull from the files the cash vouchers (along with supporting materials) for all items listed in schedule G-1. He did so and summarized all the information from those vouchers for you in Exhibit 7. (The information in Exhibit 7 is being provided to you in lieu of the actual client documents. Treat this information as though it were the documents belonging to the client and not the auditor.) You may assume that all vouchers have been properly approved and have the appropriate supporting materials attached. You may assume that you traced each vouchered invoice to the accounts payable subsidiary ledger and the January cash disbursements journal and found no discrepancies.

As part of your search for unrecorded liabilities you reviewed the voucher register and cash disbursements journal for the period January 1 through January 9. You also examined the unmatched invoice and receiver file from January 1 to January 23, 2004. You may assume that none of the January disbursements from January 10 through January 23 were applicable to the year under audit; no unmatched invoices or receiving reports for the period January 1 to January 23, 2004 were applicable to 2003.

Exhibit 8 includes an excerpt from the receiving log for December showing the last receiving reports for the year. Also included in this exhibit are the voucher register for January 1 to January 9, as well as the receiving log for that same period. You should examine the transactions recorded in these two records to determine whether the company has recorded purchases of merchandise and services in the proper period. You may assume that all the information in the receiving log is correct.

You sent confirmations to Fruit Scents, Inc. and Fruit Juicy Perfume Company. These confirmations are included in the working papers referenced G-3 and G-4, respectively.

Search for Other Unrecorded Liabilities

The search for unrecorded liabilities consists of a search for (1) unrecorded accounts payable and (2) a search for other unrecorded liabilities. You should perform the search for unrecorded *accounts payable* in this assignment documenting your evidence on working paper G-2. Defer the search for *other unrecorded liabilities* until Assignment #12, *Completing the Audit*.

To complete your search for other unrecorded liabilities, you and/or your assistant did the following:

1. Obtained a letter concerning pending litigation from the client's attorneys, Edwards, Overstreet, and Gilley. The letter is in the working papers referenced A.L./G-5. (This working paper is included in Assignment #12, *Completing the Audit.*)

2. Obtained a written representation from client management regarding liabilities and other matters. The letter is in the working papers referenced L.O.R./G-6. (This working paper is included in Assignment #12, *Completing the Audit.*)

3. Reviewed bank confirmations for possible note liabilities or contingencies. The bank confirmations are in the Assignment #3 working papers, referenced A-2 and A-4.

4. Reviewed the minutes from meetings of the Board of Directors searching for debt authorization or other liabilities.

5. Reviewed certain operating accounts, such as interest and professional fees looking for possible unrecorded note obligations, litigation contingencies, etc. (Assume that you found none.)

Note that as you perform your search for unrecorded liabilities, work performed and evidence collected in other assignments can be applicable. There may be items in other assignments (not detailed here) that relate to your search for unrecorded liabilities. After you have completed the audit, you should prepare a memorandum documenting your findings regarding unrecorded liabilities (see Assignment #12). A form for that memo is provided in the Assignment #12 working papers (referenced G-7) as an optional exercise. You should wait until Assignment #12 to complete the search for other unrecorded liabilities.

Exercises

PART A–Control Risk Analysis (Optional Exercises)

1. Prepare an internal control systems flowchart for the Accounts Payable Processing system. Use form P-7 or software. The headings for this flowchart have been provided for you on this form. Remember that the Accounts Payable Processing system is a continuation of the process that was initiated in the purchases cycle. In your flowchart, show the flow of documentation, the steps involved in the process, and note any internal control features.

2. Analyze the control procedures (strengths) related to accounts payable processing. For each strength, describe how you could test the strength. Keep in mind the control procedure categories. Use form CSF-5. Classify the control procedures according to the six categories (see General Instructions and Preparations).

3. For each weakness you find, list the weakness, a possible error or irregularity that may occur because of the weakness, and a compensating substantive test of transactions or balances to detect the error or irregularity, assuming the necessary records and documents are available to you. Use form CWF-5. Classify the weaknesses according to the six control procedure categories. You should keep these weaknesses in mind, as well as the financial statement assertions, as you write the substantive audit steps in your programs.

4. Prepare a system program for the Accounts Payable Processing System. Your program should consist of (1) tests of controls; (2) substantive tests of details of transactions; and/or (3) dual-purpose tests having both test of controls and substantive aspects. Utilize the analysis of strengths and weaknesses to guide you in preparing your program, while remembering to keep the financial statement assertions in mind. Write your program on form SP-5. Write the appropriate steps under the following headings in your program: Tests of Controls, Dual-Purpose Tests, and Substantive Tests of Transactions.

PART B–Required Exercises: Substantive Procedures

1. Prepare a substantive audit program for Accounts Payable Balances and Unrecorded Liabilities.

   The construction of your audit program for accounts payable balances and unrecorded liabilities should begin with an explicit recognition of the five financial statement assertions: (1) existence or occurrence, (2) completeness, (3) rights and obligations, (4) valuation or allocation, and (5) presentation and disclosure. You should derive your specific audit objectives concerning accounts payable balances and unrecorded liabilities from these assertions.

   Your audit program should address the five financial statement assertions, as well as any weaknesses you have found in the control structure. In this regard, keep in mind the six control procedure categories. You may assume that you have satisfied yourself as to any assertions not specifically mentioned in the narrative.

   As you write your program, remember the generalized evidence-gathering procedures of (1) recalculation, (2) physical observation, (3) confirmation, (4) verbal inquiry, (5) vouching of documents, (6) tracing, (7) scanning, and (8) analytical procedures. Use them to help you write the specific evidence-gathering procedures in your program.

Use form AP-7 to write your program. Use the financial statement assertions as the major headings in your program and list the appropriate audit steps under each of these captions.

2. Review the prior year's working papers referenced G-1 to G-4, the Permanent File material related to accounts payable, as well as the internal control questionnaire. After reviewing this material, perform the necessary audit work on working paper G-1 and prepare a schedule similar to G-2 in the prior year's working papers. Also perform any necessary audit work on schedules G-3 and G-4. (Work on schedules G-5 through G-8 is deferred to Assignment #12, *Completing the Audit*.)

APPLE BLOSSOM COLOGNE COMPANY

P-7

Accounts Payable Processing System

Purchasing Agent	Accounts Payable Clerk	Purchasing Agent	Treasurer

APPLE BLOSSOM COLOGNE COMPANY CSF-5

Accounts Payable Processing System
Internal Control Strengths

Strength	Possible Test of Controls

APPLE BLOSSOM COLOGNE COMPANY CWF-5

Accounts Payable Processing System
Internal control Weaknesses

Weakness	Potential Error	Compensating Substantive Procedure

APPLE BLOSSOM COLOGNE COMPANY **SP-5**

Accounts Payable Processing System
Program

Substantive Audit Program–Accounts Payable Balances and Unrecorded Liabilities

Assertions

Begin with the list of assertions below and add others you think appropriate. Then write your audit program to test those assertions.

1. All material liabilities are recorded.
2. All important contingencies are either provided for in the accounts or disclosed in footnotes.
3. Terms, conditions, and restrictions relating to debt are adequately disclosed.
4. Liabilities are properly classified as to their contingent or direct nature.
5. Liabilities are properly classified as to their current or long-term status.

Program Steps

Exhibit 7

Apple Blossom Cologne Company

Cash Vouchers for Accounts Payable--2003

(with supporting materials attached)

2003 Vo. No.	Vendor	Item	Discount	Terms Freight	Cost	Vendor's Invoice Date	Receiving Report Date	Date Paid	Amount Paid
12-08	A to Z Janitorial	Fee for janitorial work	Net 30	- - -	125	12-5-03	- - -	1-2-04	125
12-10	Hart Murphy Office Outfitters	See voucher in property, plant, and equipment section			8400	12-10-03	12-10-03	1-7-04	8400
12-15	Norton Exterminators	Pest control	Net 30	- - -	70	12-16-03	- - -	1-8-04	70
12-21	Fruit Juicy Perfume Co.	See voucher in inventory section			109120	12-24-03	12-29-03	1-8-04	109120
12-31	Apple Valley Security Systems	Security survey	Net 30	- - -	85	12-26-03	- - -	1-9-04	1485
12-34	Edwards, Overstreet & Gilley	Retainer and legal fees	Net 30	- - -	4820	12-26-03	- - -	1-9-04	4820
12-35	Fruit Scents, Inc.	See voucher in inventory section			12480	12-29-03	12-30-03	1-9-04	11080
12-42	Flash Freight Co.	See voucher in inventory section			400	12-29-03	- - -	1-9-04	400
12-43	Dr. Edward Abel	Plant injury	Net 30	- - -	50	12-26-03	- - -	1-9-04	50

EXHIBIT 8

APPLE BLOSSOM COLOGNE COMPANY

Receiving Log
December 2003

Date Shipped	Receiving Date	Receiver No.	Vendor	Description	Terms
12-24-03	12-29-03	12-10	Fruit Juicy Perfume Co.	800 cases Skin Tone Lotion 400 cases Hand Crème	FOB, Chi
12-29-03	12-30-03	12-11	Fruit Scents, Inc.	100 cases Lemon Oil	FOB, Hope
12-30-03	12-31-03	12-12	Fruit Juicy Perfume Co.	150 cases Face Creme	FOB, Chi

APPLE BLOSSOM COLOGNE COMPANY

Receiving Log
January 2004

Date Shipped	Receiving Date	Receiver No.	Vendor	Description	Terms
12-26-03	1-2-04	1-01	Fruit Juicy Perfume Co.	60 cases Skin Tone Lotion	FOB, Chi
12-29-03	1-5-04	1-02	Fruit Scents, Inc.	100 cases R320 Apple Oil	FOB, Hope
12-31-03	1-9-04	1-03	Fruit Juicy Perfume Co.	50 cases Skin Tone Lotion	FOB, Chi

EXHIBIT 8 (Continued)

APPLE BLOSSOM COLOGNE COMPANY

Voucher Register
January 2004

Date	Voucher No.	Name	Explanation	Acct #	Amount
1-2-04	1-1	Central Power & Light Co.	Electric service 11/15 to 12/22	830	1100.00
1-2-04	1-2	William F. Reimann	Truck repairs	828	468.00
1-2-04	1-3	Fruit Juicy Perfume Co.	Receiver No. 1-01	109	5184.00
1-2-04	1-4	Hoffmann Supply Co.	Conveyor belts	828	240.00
1-5-04	1-5	Fulton Paper Co.	Copying paper	824	620.00
1-6-04	1-6	Fruit Juicy Perfume Co.	Receiver No. 12-12	109	15480.00
1-6-04	1-7	A to Z Janitorial	Services for December	832	230.00
1-8-04	1-8	Flash Freight Co.	Freight for merchandise on rec. 1-02 Invoice dated 12/29/03	109	400.00
1-8-04	1-9	Fruit Scents, Inc.	Receiver No. 1-02	109	33440.00
1-9-04	1-10	Steck Hamilton Office Supplies	Office supplies	824	1400.00
1-9-04	1-11	Petrozine Fuel Co.	Fuel oil	830	850.00
1-9-04	1-12	Fruit Juicy Perfume Co.	Receiver No. 1-03	109	4320.00

Apple Blossom Cologne Company G-1

Accounts Payable

12-31-03

(Prepared by client)

Vo. No.	Vendor		Amount	
12-08	A to Z Janitorial		125	
12-10	Hart Murphy Office Outfitters		8400	
12-15	Norton Exterminators		70	
12-21	Fruit Juicy Perfume Co.		109120	
12-31	Apple Valley Security		1485	
12-34	Edwards, Overstreet & Gilley		4820	
12-35	Fruit Scents, Inc.		11080	
12-42	Flash Freight Co.		400	
12-43	Dr. Edward Abel		50	
			135550	

Apple Blossom Cologne Company

1308 Bee Hive Boulevard • Chicago, Illinois 60615
Phone: 312-477-7288
Fax: 312-477-9999
Internet: www.appleblossom.com

January 2, 2004
Fruit Scents, Inc.
5913 Overland Drive
Hope, Michigan 48628

Dear Sir or Madam:
Will you please confirm the amount owed to you by us at the close of business December 31, 2003. Please complete and return this itemized statement directly to our auditors, Anderson, Olds, and Watershed, Certified Public Accountants. A return envelope addressed to our auditors is enclosed for your convenience. We appreciate your prompt attention to this matter.

Amount currently due $44,520

Amount past due ______

Collateral amount ______

Comments Margaret Granahan
Controller

Very truly yours,

APPLE BLOSSOM COLOGNE COMPANY

Parker Shelton

Parker Shelton

Controller

Apple Blossom Cologne Company

1308 Bee Hive Boulevard • Chicago, Illinois 60615
Phone: 312-477-7288
Fax: 312-477-9999
Internet: www.appleblossom.com

January 2, 2004
Fruit Juicy Perfume Company
4404 Riverdale Avenue
Springfield, Missouri 65801

Dear Sir or Madam:
Will you please confirm the amount owed to you by us at the close of business December 31, 2003. Please complete and return this itemized statement directly to our auditors, Anderson, Olds, and Watershed, Certified Public Accountants. A return envelope addressed to our auditors is enclosed for your convenience. We appreciate your prompt attention to this matter.

Amount currently due $124,600

Amount past due ______

Collateral amount ______

Comments Arthur Jones
Chief Accountant
Fruit Juicy Perfume Company

Very truly yours,
APPLE BLOSSOM COLOGNE COMPANY
Parker Shelton
Parker Shelton
Controller

Assignment #9
Payroll Processing and Accrued Liabilities

The information that follows is grouped into two categories: 1) Internal Control and 2) Substantive Audit Procedures. This information is to be used to complete the exercises for this assignment. Do the optional exercises only if told to do so by your instructor.

Relevant Information

Internal Control

Review the internal control questionnaire completed for you by Jasper Parsons. As you read through the questionnaire, keep in mind the six categories of control procedures: (1) segregation of duties, (2) access, (3) authorization, (4) input controls, (5) processing controls, and (6) output controls. Then try to determine the possible errors or irregularities that could occur. Note that the most important controls over payroll are an adequate segregation of functions and proper supervision. Your firm has found that the personnel involved in the payroll area are generally competent.

Possible errors or irregularities in the payroll area include:

1. Wages, salaries, and related amounts may have been debited to the wrong account.
2. Payroll may have been incorrectly calculated.
3. Hours may have been recorded incorrectly and payments made for work not performed.
4. Employees may have been underpaid and payroll therefore understated.
5. Employees may have been overpaid (e.g., incorrect wage rate) and payroll therefore overstated.
6. Fictitious employees may have been included on the payroll.

Internal Control Questionnaire--Payroll System

	Yes	*No*	*Comments*
1. Are the personnel, timekeeping, payroll, and disbursement functions independent?	_	√	Timekeeping and personnel functions are performed by Louise McWhorter.
2. Does the person who handles the personnel records notify the payroll clerk of personnel changes?	√	_	
3. Are checks prepared by personnel who do not prepare payroll or have access to the payroll records?	√	_	
4. Are the checks signed by personnel who do not have access to the payroll records?	_	√	Controller signs checks, also has access to payroll records.
5. Is a timeclock employed for hourly employees?	√	_	

	Yes	No	Remarks
6. Are time cards and time reports approved by supervisors?	√	–	
7. Are all hires and terminations approved by a responsible official?	√	–	President initials
8. Are all wage rates approved by a responsible official?	√	–	President initials
9. Are all employees paid by checks that are prenumbered?	√	–	
10. Is the payroll recalculated for mechanical accuracy as to hours worked, wage rates, and deductions?	√	–	Payroll software is used.
11. Does a responsible official approve the payroll prior to payment?	√	–	Treasurer initials.
12. Are paychecks distributed by someone who has no other payroll responsibilities?	√	–	
13. Is a separate payroll bank account employed?	√	–	
14. Is this account reconciled by someone who does not have payroll responsibilities?	–	√	Reconciliation is performed by treasurer, who also signs checks.

Substantive Audit Procedures--Accrued Liabilities

At December 31, 2003, Apple Blossom Cologne Company had several types of accrued liabilities. Each of them is a different account and each is treated separately below. Study the 2002 working papers before you begin your audit work.

Accrued Payrolls and Payroll Taxes

An analysis of the Accrued Payroll Taxes accounts has been prepared by Donald McKenna. This schedule is referenced H-1 in the working papers.

Salaried employees are paid on the first day of every month for the previous month's work. Since January 1 is a holiday, payday for salaried employees was Friday, January 2. Hourly employees are paid each week on Friday for the previous week's work. The hourly employees' time is spread evenly over a 5-day week, Monday through Friday.

Gross wages and salaries for 2003 were $1,618,643. The company had between 35 and 41 employees throughout the first three quarters of the year. From the beginning of the fourth quarter through the end of the year, Apple Blossom had 38 employees. During the year there was one employee earning in excess of $76,200 annually. The total excess, which is not subject to F.I.C.A. taxes, amounted to $129,500. All 41 employees who worked for Apple Blossom during 2003 exceeded the $7,000 maximum salary base for unemployment taxes.

Apple Blossom did not set up an accrual for payrolls and payroll taxes on either (1) the salaried employees for the month of December, to be paid in January, or (2) the hourly employees for the pay period ending December 26 (to be paid on January 2, 2004) and the "stub period" December 29th through 31st. This latter "stub period" is included in the hourly employees' wages paid on January 9, 2004. For such accruals, the net payroll is credited to the Wages and Salaries Payable account. Withheld income tax, medicare, and F.I.C.A. tax, along with the employer portion of F.I.C.A. tax and medicare, are credited to Accrued Payroll Taxes. Unemployment taxes are also credited to the Accrued Payroll Taxes account.

The following tax rates were applicable for 2003; the rates will remain the same in 2004:

State unemployment	3.8% of first $7,000 of wages
Federal unemployment	0.8% of first $7,000 of wages
F.I.C.A.	6.2% of first $76,200 of wages (employer matches the 6.2% withheld from employee)
Medicare	1.45% of wages (employer matches the 1.45% withheld)
Federal income tax withheld	15% (Income tax withheld and F.I.C.A. tax withheld are rounded to the nearest dollar on each employee.)

Apple Blossom Cologne Company makes quarterly payments for the accrued payroll tax liability by depositing the accrued amount at a local bank, which is a depository for federal taxes. For the payments shown on schedule H-1, you may assume that you have (1) traced them to the cash disbursements journal, (2) examined the paid vouchers and supporting materials, and (3) vouched the amounts to employer copies of Form 941, Employer's Quarterly Federal Tax Return, and to federal and state unemployment tax forms. Apple Blossom files these forms within a month after the close of each quarter.

You may assume that during the test of transactions work you checked the payroll register and the personnel records and noted the following gross amounts due the salaried employees each month of 2003. All 24 of the salaried employees listed were employed by Apple Blossom Cologne Company for the full year of 2003.

Administration

President (Lancaster)	$11,008
Secretary (McWhorter)	3,450
Mail clerk (Klett)	1,492

Sales and Credit

Sales manager (Jacobs)	$7,133
Credit manager (Robertson)	4,333
Six salespersons (each)	4,675
Accounts receivable clerk (Swift)	2,067

Plant Operations

Production superintendent (Brown)	$7,525
Foreman (Freitag)	4,733
Purchasing agent (Palmer)	3,775
Receiving manager (Beauchamp)	3,775
Repackaging manager (Doyle)	4,725
Shipping manager (Evershock)	4,525
Inventory clerk (Columbo)	2,008

Controller

Controller (Shelton)	$7,008
Bookkeeper (McKenna)	3,817
Accounts payable clerk (Dull)	1,550

Treasurer

Treasurer (Stockton)	$7,217
Cashier (Lewis)	2,300

In computing the hourly employees' wages payable at year-end, the gross amount for the week ended December 26, 2003, was $7,938 for the 14 hourly employees.

Dividends Payable

Dividends are declared by the Board of Directors and recorded in the minutes of the Board meetings. You have examined the minutes of Board meetings and your documentation of those minutes is filed in the Permanent File section of this audit case. You may assume that you traced the dividend payment to the cash disbursements journal in January 2004.

Property Taxes Payable

In the state of Illinois, city and county property taxes are levied against personal and real property (inventory and fixed assets) owned by a company as of January 1 of each year. Both the city of Chicago and Cook County tax assessors mail out property tax bills in October. They are due by the following January 31. You have checked with the city and county tax assessors to determine the assessment bases and tax rates.

For the city of Chicago, assessed value is 75% of the following property: inventory, land, and depreciated value of depreciable fixed assets. The tax rate is $1.40 per $100 of assessed value.

Cook County assessed value is 27% of the following property: inventory, land, and the depreciated value of depreciable fixed assets. The tax rate is $1.01 per $100 of assessed value. You were able to trace the payment made during 2003 (voucher #1-14) and in January 2004, to the cash disbursements journal.

Exercises

PART A–Control Risk Analysis (Optional Exercises)

1. From the information provided in the Permanent File and the internal control questionnaire, prepare a flowchart of Apple Blossom's Payroll Processing System. Use form P-8 or software. Show the flow of documentation, the steps involved in the process, and note any internal control features.

2. Describe the control procedures (strengths) related to payroll processing. For each strength, list a test of controls you could perform to test the effectiveness of the control. Remember to think about the six categories of control procedures. Using form CSF-6, classify the strengths according to these six categories (see General Instructions and Preparations).

3. For each weakness you find, list the weakness, a potential error or irregularity that may occur because of the weakness, as well as a compensating substantive test of transactions or balances to detect the error or irregularity, assuming the necessary records and documents are available to you. Use form CWF-6. Classify the weaknesses according to the six categories of control procedures.

4. Prepare a formal program consisting of tests of controls and substantive tests of details of transactions for the payroll processing system. Use form SP-6. Your program may consist of dual-purpose tests having both test of controls and substantive aspects. Keep in mind the financial statement assertions. (Example: "Payroll transactions represent expenditures for bona fide services received by the company.") Use the following major captions for your program: Tests of Controls, Dual-Purpose Tests, and Substantive Tests of Transactions. List the appropriate audit steps under each of these headings.

PART B–Required Exercises: Substantive Procedures

1. Prepare a substantive audit program to test accrued liabilities. The construction of an audit program for accrued liability transactions and balances should begin with an explicit recognition of the five financial statement assertions: (1) existence or occurrence, (2) completeness, (3) rights and obligations, (4) valuation or allocation, and (5) presentation and disclosure. You should derive your specific audit objectives from these assertions. Your audit program should address the five financial statement assertions, as well as any weaknesses you have found in the control structure. In this regard, keep in mind the six categories of control procedures. You may assume that you have satisfied yourself as to any assertions not specifically mentioned in the narrative.

   As you write your program, remember the generalized evidence-gathering procedures of (1) recalculation, (2) physical observation, (3) confirmation, (4) verbal inquiry, (5) vouching of documents, (6) tracing, (7) scanning, and (8) analytical procedures. Use them to help you write the specific evidence-gathering procedures in your program.

   Use form AP-8. Use the financial statement assertions as your major captions. List the appropriate audit steps under each of these headings.

2. Study the prior year's working papers, schedules H-1 through H-3. Prepare a working paper similar to H-1 in the prior year's working papers to audit the accrued payroll taxes and employer payroll tax expense.

   Prepare a schedule similar to H-2 in the prior year's working papers. Employees' federal income tax withheld by Apple Blossom averaged 15% per employee. Remember that, since the salaries and wages are paid in January, employees will be starting a new tax year. The applicable payroll taxes pertaining thereto should be accrued in December.

   Study working paper H-3 in the prior period's working papers. Prepare a similar schedule for the current year, referenced H-3, to analyze the accounts, Dividends Payable and Accrued Property Taxes.

APPLE BLOSSOM COLOGNE COMPANY
Payroll System Flowchart

P-8

Plant and Office	Personnel	Payroll Clerk	Purchasing Agent	Treasurer

APPLE BLOSSOM COLOGNE COMPANY CSF-6

Payroll System
Internal Control Strengths

Strength	Possible Test of Controls

APPLE BLOSSOM COLOGNE COMPANY CWF-6

Payroll System
Internal control Weaknesses

Weakness	Potential Error	Compensating Substantive Procedure

Payroll Program

Substantive Audit Program–Accrued Liabilities

Assertions

Begin with the list of assertions below and add others you think appropriate. Then write your audit program to test those assertions.

1. All material accrued liabilities are recorded.
2. All important contingencies are either provided for in the accounts or disclosed in footnotes.
3. Accrued liabilities are properly classified as to their as to their current or long-term status.

Apple Blossom Cologne Company — H-1

Accrued Payroll Taxes

12-31-03

(Prepared by client)

	Balance 12-31-02	Additions	Pay-ments	Balance 12-31-03
F.I.C.A. Tax	43,879	184,654	194,960	33,573
Medicare	10,553	46,940	48,958	8,535
State Unemployment	3,992	10,108	14,100	-0-
Federal Unemployment	840	2,128	2,968	-0-
Withholding Tax	54,582	242,796	253,233	44,145
Balance per client	113,846	486,626	514,219	86,253

Assignment #10
Notes Payable and Accrued Interest

The information that follows is grouped into two categories: (1) Internal Control and (2) Substantive Audit Procedures. This information is to be used to complete the exercises.

Relevant Information

Internal Control

The following internal control questionnaire was completed by Jasper Parsons on December 15, 2003. Review this questionnaire before you write your audit program for notes payable related transactions and balances. As you go through the questionnaire, keep in mind the six categories of control procedures: (1) segregation of functions, (2) access, (3) authorization, (4) input controls, (5) processing controls, and (6) output controls. Then try to think of potential errors or irregularities that could occur.

Internal Control Questionnaire–Notes Payable and Accrued Interest

		Yes	*No*	*Comments*
1.	Is specific authority to obligate the company separated from the actual recording of debt transactions?	√	_	Treasurer has authority to obligate. Controller records.
2.	Are all borrowings authorized by the board of directors?	√	_	
3.	Are paid notes cancelled and stamped "paid?"	√	_	
4.	Are detailed records of borrowings maintained by an employee who is not authorized to sign checks or notes?	√	_	Kept by Don McKenna.
5.	Does the accounting department review accruals of interest on all debt instruments?	√	_	
6.	Are interest payments reconciled with notes on hand?	_	√	

Substantive Audit Procedures: Notes Payable And Accrued Interest

At December 31, 2003, Apple Blossom Cologne Company had a note payable outstanding to the Midwestern Mutual Life Insurance Company in the amount of $475,000. You have received a confirmation of the note and terms from Midwestern. The confirmation is included in the working papers. The letter of confirmation from Midwestern Mutual is referenced I-2.

Study the notes payable and accrued interest schedule included in the prior year's working papers. That schedule is referenced I-1. You have received a confirmation from Midwestern Mutual Life Insurance Company, referenced I-2 and included with the materials in this assignment. You may assume that the data in this confirmation agrees with the client's copy of the note, which you have examined. For the $125,000 note to the Big City National, you were able to trace the $140,938 payment for principal and interest into the cash disbursements journal dated April 30, 2003 (voucher 4-38). You may also assume you were able to verify this information with the bank by means of a standard bank confirmation.

The only assets subject to lien with respect to the long-term debt are those indicated in the confirmation. Apple Blossom has made no provision for funding the long-term debt.

Required Exercises

1. Prepare a substantive audit program for Notes Payable and Accrued Interest.

   The construction of an audit program for notes payable transactions and balances should begin with the auditor's explicit recognition of the five financial statement assertions: (1) existence or occurrence, (2) completeness, (3) rights and obligations, (4) valuation or allocation, and (5) presentation and disclosure. You should derive your specific audit objectives for notes payable and accrued interest from these assertions.

   Your audit program should address the five financial statement assertions, as well as any weakness in the system of internal control. In this regard, keep in mind the six categories of control procedures. You may assume that you have satisfied yourself as to any assertions not specifically mentioned in the narrative.

   As you write your program, remember the generalized evidence-gathering procedures of (1) recalculation, (2) physical observation, (3) confirmation, (4) verbal inquiry, (5) vouching of documents, (6) tracing, (7) scanning, and (8) analytical procedures. Use them to help you write the specific evidence-gathering procedures in your program.

   Use form AP-9 to write your program. Use the financial statement assertions as your program headings. List the appropriate audit steps under each of these captions.

2. Prepare a schedule similar to schedule I-1 for the current year, performing all required audit work. Also make any notations on I-2 that you deem necessary.

Substantive Audit Program–Notes Payable and Accrued Interest

Assertions

Begin with the list of assertions below and add others you think appropriate. Then write your audit program to test those assertions.

1. All material debt liabilities are recorded.
2. Debt liabilities are properly classified as to their contingent or direct nature.
3. Debt liabilities are properly classified as to their current or long-term status.
4. Terms, conditions, and restrictions relating to debt are adequately disclosed.

Program Steps

MIDWESTERN MUTUAL LIFE INSURANCE COMPANY

834 O'Keefe Street
Chicago, Illinois 60614

January 19, 2004
Anderson, Olds and Watershed
Certified Public Accountants
615 Big City National Bank Building
Main at Michigan Avenue
Chicago, Illinois 60612

At the request of Mr. Parker Shelton of the Apple Blossom Cologne Company, we confirm to you that the company was indebted to us on December 31, 2003 in the following manner:

> Note dated August 31, 2003: Principal amount of $475,000 due August 31, 2010. Interest at 10% payable on August 31st of each year. The note is secured by plant machinery and equipment as listed in chattel mortgage dated August 31, 2003.

Please let us know if we can be of further assistance.

Sincerely,

William H. McHale

William H. McHale
Loan Officer

WHM/caw

Assignment #11
Capital Stock and Retained Earnings

The information that follows is grouped into two categories: 1) Internal Control and 2) Substantive Audit Procedures. This information is to be used to complete the exercises for this assignment. Do the optional exercises only if told to do so by your instructor.

Relevant Information

Internal Control

The following internal control questionnaire was completed by Jasper Parsons. Before you write your substantive audit program for equity transactions and balances, review the questionnaire to determine strengths and weaknesses in the control procedures related to equity transactions and balances. Keep in mind the six control procedure categories as you go through the questionnaire: (1) segregation of functions, (2) access, (3) authorization, (4) input controls, (5) processing controls, and (6) output controls. Then determine potential errors or irregularities that could occur.

Internal Control Questionnaire–Capital Stock and Retained Earnings

		Yes	*No*	*Comments*
1.	Is an independent registrar and transfer agent employed?	_	√	Stock transfers handled by corporate secretary
2.	Is an independent dividend agent employed?	_	√	Checks paid through regular bank account.
3.	Are unissued stock certificates kept under the control of a responsible official?	√	_	Corporate secretary.
4.	Are stock certificates prenumbered?	√	_	
5.	Are cancelled stock certificates properly voided and retained in the stock certificate book?	√	_	
6.	Is a subsidiary ledger of stockholders maintained?	√	_	By bookkeeper
7.	Are the certificate book and stockholder ledger reconciled to the control account periodically?	_	√	With few transactions, periodic reconciliation is not considered necessary. Bookkeeper reconciles all records when capital transactions occur.

Substantive Audit Procedures–Transactions and Balances

Before beginning your work on the Capital Stock and Retained Earnings accounts, study the prior year's working papers. The working paper memorandum indexed J-1 is an analysis of the Capital Stock and Other Contributed Capital accounts, while an analysis of the Retained Earnings account is provided on K-1.

When Apple Blossom Cologne Company was incorporated in 1991, 20,000 shares of $100 par value common stock were authorized. As of January 1, 2003, 9,250 shares of the 20,000 authorized were issued and outstanding. (Refer to history and background in *Permanent File*.) No additional shares were issued in 2003. You were able to verify this through examination of corporate minutes, the stock certificate book, stockholder subsidiary ledger, and cash receipts and disbursements journals. The company has never repurchased any of its own stock.

Because Apple Blossom Cologne Company is a small corporation and stock transactions are few, the company does not employ the services of a stock registrar or transfer agent. Stock records are kept in the stock certificate book and stockholder subsidiary ledger. You reviewed these records and accounted for all issued and unissued stock certificates.

You may assume that your discussions with the client indicated that no stock options, warrants, rights, or conversion privileges existed at year-end.

Required Exercises

1. Prepare a substantive audit program for capital stock and retained earnings transactions and balances. The construction of an audit program for equity transactions and balances should begin with an explicit recognition of the five financial statement assertions: (1) existence or occurrence, (2) completeness, (3) rights and obligations, (4) valuation or allocation, and (5) presentation and disclosure. From these assertions, you should derive your specific audit objectives.

   Your audit program should address the financial statement assertions, as well as any weaknesses in the internal control structure. In this regard, keep in mind the six control procedure categories. You may assume that you have satisfied yourself as to any assertions not specifically mentioned in the narrative.

   As you write your program, remember the generalized evidence-gathering procedures of (1) recalculation, (2) physical observation, (3) confirmation, (4) verbal inquiry, (5) vouching of documents, (6) tracing, (7) scanning, and (8) analytical procedures. Use them to help write the specific evidence-gathering procedures in your program.

   Write your program on Form AP-10. Use the financial statement assertions as the major headings in your program. List the appropriate audit steps under each of these captions.

2. After studying the prior year's working papers, J-1 and K-1, prepare similar working papers for the current year. You should prepare the retained earnings schedule (K-1) showing the balance in Retained Earnings per client. Use the amounts before audit adjustments. Starting with the beginning balance of retained earnings at 1/1/03, subtract dividends and add net income. (After you correct net income for your audit adjustments and their tax effect, you will have to adjust the retained earnings schedule. See Assignment #12, *Completing the Audit*.)

Audit Program–Capital Stock and Retained Earnings

Assertions

Begin with the list of assertions below and add others you think appropriate. Then write your audit program to test those assertions.

1. Dividends declared by the Board of Directors have been properly recorded and paid.
2. Treasury stock transactions are properly accounted for and disclosed.
3. Capital stock terms and features are adequately disclosed.
4. Options, warrants, and other stock issue plans are properly accounted for and disclosed.
5. Restrictions on retained earnings are properly disclosed.

Program Steps

Assignment #12
Completing the Audit

In every audit engagement, the reputation of your audit firm is on the line. It is therefore extremely important that you, as the auditor-in-charge, assure that the audit has been performed with the utmost care, that no material misstatements remain, and that the financial statements are materially correct in all respects. Auditing textbooks are replete with accounts of auditors who were successfully sued because they failed to follow up on unusual items discovered during the audit. The audit completion phase is the last opportunity to tie up loose ends. To complete the audit, a number of miscellaneous items remain. Use the information provided to complete the exercises in this assignment. *Do the optional exercises only if told to do so by your instructor.*

Operating Accounts

Many of the operations accounts have been examined during your completion of Assignments 2 through 11. For example, insurance expense, rent expense, and other miscellaneous expenses were tested in the prepaid expense assignment (#5). Depreciation expense was tested in the fixed assets work (Assignment #7), while interest expense was examined in Assignment #10, and so forth. You may assume that all operations accounts not examined by you during your completion of Assignments 2 through 11 (e.g., Sales and Cost of Sales, etc.) have been examined by an assistant working on the Apple Blossom Cologne Company audit under your supervision. The assistant examined the accounts for unusual items, significant monthly trends, and so on. You may assume that the work revealed no items of an unusual nature and no proposed adjustments. You are satisfied that your assistant performed an adequate investigation of those accounts.

Analytical Procedures

Auditing standards require the auditor to perform analytical procedures at the end of the audit to provide an overall review of the financial information and to determine the effect of audit adjustments on the comparisons and ratios. Assume you performed this analysis and determined that the effect of your adjustments did not have a significant impact on the premises used for planning the engagement.

Required Exercises

1. **Federal Income Tax and Retained Earnings Working Papers**

   To determine the federal income taxes payable, apply the tax rate to net income before taxes (after audit adjustments). You may assume that there are no differences between tax income and accounting income. The following tax rates are applicable:

   On first $50,000 of income .... rate is 15%
   On next $25,000 of income .... rate is 25%
   On income over $75,000 .... rate is 34%

   Study schedule H-4 in the prior year's working papers. Donald McKenna has prepared a similar schedule referenced H-4 for the current year. You may assume that you were able to trace all payments and deposits against the client's tax liability to the cash disbursements journal. You also examined each of the paid vouchers and were able to agree the amounts paid during 2002 and 2003 with the client's copy of the tax return. All the client's tax returns are prepared by your audit firm.

Required. After posting your adjusting entries to the working trial balance, determine the addition to or reduction of the federal income taxes recorded by the client. Perform all required audit work on schedule H-4 for the current year. Then post any required adjusting entry for income taxes to the trial balance.

In Assignment #11, you prepared the retained earnings schedule K-1 showing the balance in Retained Earnings before your audit adjustments. After you correct net income for your audit adjustments, you will have to update the retained earnings schedule also.

Required. Complete the retained earnings schedule (K-1). To obtain the ending balance of retained earnings per audit, adjust the ending balance per client for the net effect of your audit adjustments as found in the totals of the "Adjustments" column on TB-IS.

2. Working Trial Balances

Required. All audit adjustments should be posted to the schedule of adjusting journal entries, working paper AJE, as well as the working trial balances, working papers TB-BS and TB-IS. Each adjustment should also be documented on the working paper that gave rise to it. After posting all adjustments, add across to obtain the trial balance per audit. Any reclassification entries affecting financial statement presentation should be posted to working paper RJE and to the trial balance. After posting these adjustments to the trial balance, add across.

3. Minutes from Meetings of Board of Directors

Excerpts of minutes of meetings of the Board of Directors are provided in the Permanent File working papers.

Required. Examine the cross-referencing on the prior year's minutes. Items of accounting import should be similarly referenced to appropriate places in the current year's working papers. The excerpts from the minutes of Board meetings should remain as part of the Permanent File located immediately after the chart of accounts.

4. Assembling the Working Papers

Required. After you have completed all your audit work, assemble your working papers in the following order:

Current File

(1) Senior's Audit Memorandum (an optional assignment)
(2) Planning working papers (from Assignment #1)
(3) Draft of audit report (an optional assignment)
(4) Draft of financial statements and footnotes (an optional assignment)
(5) Letter concerning deficiencies in the internal control structure (an optional assignment)
(6) Working trial balances–balance sheet and income statement
(7) Schedule of adjusting journal entries
(8) Assignment working papers in working paper order (A, B, C, etc.); include internal control analysis (if applicable) and audit program(s) with the assignment's working papers.

(1) History and Background
(2) Organization Chart and Organizational Structure
(3) Flowcharts (optional assignments)
(4) Internal Control Structure Narratives
(5) Chart of Accounts
(6) Minutes of Meetings of Board of Directors.

After you have assembled your working papers in the file folder, review them a final time for cleaning up last minute details like cross-referencing, tying out, and completing explanations. Finally, turn your working papers in for the partner's review.

Optional Exercises

1. **Attorney's Letter**

You have requested and received from the client's attorneys a statement regarding pending litigation, contingent liabilities, and major transactions (present or planned).

Required. You should consider the information provided in this letter and incorporate it into your audit documentation. File this letter in the liabilities working papers referenced A.L./G-5.

2. **Client's Letter of Representations**

This letter covers the client's representations to your audit firm as to asset valuation, the status of liabilities, and other matters that may affect the financial statements.

Required. Complete the client's letter of representations by filling in dollar amounts on your firm's standard representation letter form. After having Larry Lancaster and Parker Shelton review and sign the letter, file it in the working papers section with the liabilities working papers, referenced L.O.R./G-6.

3. **Contingent Liabilities and Subsequent Events Memorandum**

To insure proper disclosure, you should perform a search for contingent liabilities and subsequent events. You received a letter from the client's legal counsel; this letter provides information about contingencies. You also made inquiries of the president, controller, and treasurer. Your discussions with management revealed no additional contingencies or subsequent events.

Required. You should determine from the minutes of the Board of Directors' meetings and from other evidence available to you whether all contingent liabilities and subsequent events are properly treated. After completing your investigation, prepare a memorandum documenting your findings and conclusions. A form for that memorandum is provided and referenced G-7. This memorandum should be filed with the liabilities working papers. (Note that the audit opinion may have to be modified for material contingencies. Adjustments and/or disclosures may be required; assume that the client will adjust/disclose as you propose.)

4. **Unrecorded Liability Search Memorandum**

Required. Having completed your evidence-gathering activities for the audit, you should prepare a memorandum documenting your search for unrecorded liabilities. A form for that memo is provided in this assignment, referenced G-8. Include this memorandum with the accrued liabilities working papers.

5. **Auditor's Report**

Required. Prepare a draft of the auditor's report taking into account all information obtained from your audit work. Place the draft of the audit report immediately following the planning working papers from Assignment #1.

6. **Financial Statements and Accompanying Notes**

Required. On the working trial balances, summarize and reclassify items for financial statement presentation. Prepare a draft of the current year's financial statements, including footnote disclosures. When you assemble the final working paper folder, place your draft of the financial statements immediately following the auditor's report.

7. **Senior's Audit Memorandum**

As the senior auditor "in-charge" in the field, you are responsible for preparing an internal memorandum discussing problems that may have a significant financial and/or economic impact on the client's statements. Discuss any significant audit and/or accounting problems you encountered, how you resolved those problems (e.g., proposed an adjustment, disclosed the item, prepared an internal control letter comment, etc.), and your conclusions about the audit as a whole. This memorandum is used by the partner-in-charge as a starting point for reviewing the audit working papers.

Required. Prepare the senior's audit memorandum describing any significant problems encountered during the audit. Address this memorandum to the partner-in-charge of the Apple Blossom audit.

8. **Internal Control Structure Letter**

Generally accepted auditing standards require the auditor to communicate to senior management and the Board of Directors significant deficiencies in the design or operation of the control structure (reportable conditions). A reportable condition could adversely affect the client's ability to record, process, summarize, and report financial data, thus introducing material errors into the financial statements. Your audit firm also considers this an opportunity to improve client relations and additionally to enhance internal control in order to benefit subsequent audits.

Required. Prepare a letter pointing out any reportable conditions you have encountered, as well as your suggestions for improvement. Place this letter in the working papers after the draft of the financial statements and footnotes.

Apple Blossom Cologne Company H-4

Federal Income Taxes Payable

12-31-03

(Prepared by client)

				Tax Liability	Tax Expense
	Balance 12-31-02			63772	
	Additions: 2003 taxes			100000	100000
	Payments:			163772	
	Final payment Jan. 2003				
	on 2002 taxes		63772		
	First quarter deposit, 2003 taxes		25000		
	Second quarter deposit, 2003 taxes		25000		
	Third quarter deposit, 2003 taxes		25000	138772	
				25000	100000

A.L./G-5

Edwards, Overstreet, and Gilley

Attorneys at Law

1604 South Fourth . Chicago, Illinois 60614
Phone: 312-555-3892
Fax: 312-555-9998

January 22, 2004

Anderson, Olds and Watershed
Certified Public Accountants
615 Big City National Bank Building
Main at Michigan Avenue
Chicago, Illinois 60612

Re: Apple Blossom Cologne Company

Dear Sir or Madam:

By letter dated January 2, 2004, Mr. Lawrence Lancaster of Apple Blossom Cologne Company (The "Company") has requested us to furnish you with certain information in connection with your examination of the accounts of the Company as of December 31,2003. While this firm represents the Company on a regular basis, our engagement has been limited to specific matters as to which we were consulted by the Company.

Subject to the foregoing and to the last paragraph of this letter we advise you that since January 1,2003 we have not been engaged to give substantive attention to, or represent the Company in connection with material loss contingencies coming within the scope of clause (a) of Paragraph 5 of the Statement of Policy referred to in the last paragraph of this letter, except as follows:

We are responding to an action that has been initiated against Apple Blossom Cologne Company alleging injury due to defective products. The action, *Newman v. Apple Blossom Cologne Company,* is not in litigation. Investigation, preparation, including development of the factual data and legal research and progress of the matter have reached a stage whereby an assessment can be made, taking all relevant factors into account that may affect the outcome. Although the litigation is being defended vigorously and the Company has meritorious defenses, we are of the opinion that the plaintiff will likely prevail in this action, and it is extremely doubtful that the Company will prevail. As to the amount of potential loss, total costs and damages that might ultimately be assessed against the Company will be much less than the $100,000 damages claimed by the plaintiff. However, at this time the amount is not susceptible of reasonable estimation.

(Continued)

A.L./G-5

Page Two

The information set forth herein is as of the date of this letter and we disclaim any undertaking to advise you of changes which thereafter may be brought to our attention.

This response is limited by, and in accordance with, the ABA Statement of Policy Regarding Lawyers' Responses to Auditors' Requests for Information (December 1975); without limiting the generality of the foregoing, the limitation set forth in such Statement on the scope and use of this response (Paragraphs 2 and 7) are specifically incorporated herein by reference, and any description herein of any "loss contingencies" is qualified in its entirety by Paragraph 5 of the Statement and the accompanying Commentary (which is an integral part of the Statement). Consistent with the last sentence of Paragraph 6 of the ABA Statement of Policy and pursuant to the Company's request, this will confirm as correct the Company's understanding as set forth in its audit inquiry letter to us that whenever, in the course of performing legal services for the Company with respect to a matter recognized to involve an unasserted possible claim or assessment that may call for financial statement disclosure, we have formed a professional conclusion that the Company must disclose or consider disclosure concerning such possible claim or assessment, we, as a matter of professional responsibility to the Company, will so advise the Company and will consult with the Company concerning the question of such disclosure and the applicable requirements of Statement of Financial Accounting Standards No. 5.

Very truly yours,

EDWARDS, OVERSTREET AND GILLEY

Michael Overstreet

Michael Overstreet
Partner

Apple Blossom Cologne
Company

1308 Beehive Boulevard Chicago, Illinois 60615
Phone: 312-477-7288
Fax: 312-477-9999
Internet: www.appleblossom.com

February 4, 2004

Anderson, Olds and Watershed
Certified Public Accountants
615 Big City National Bank Building
Main at Michigan
Chicago, Illinois 60612

Gentlemen:

The following representations are made to you in connection with your examination of the balance sheet of Apple Blossom Cologne Company as of December 31, 2003, and of the statement of earnings for the year then ended. These representations are accurate to the best of our knowledge and belief.

We understand that your examination was conducted in accordance with generally accepted auditing standards and accordingly included such tests of the accounting records and such other auditing procedures as you deemed necessary in the circumstances. We also understand that your audit does not include a detailed examination of all transactions and therefore cannot be expected to disclose all irregularities should any exist.

Receivables
Trade Accounts receivable in the amount of $____________are valid receivables and do not include any amounts for goods shipped on consignment or approval. In our opinion, the balance in Allowance for Bad Debts of $_________is sufficient to cover any losses, discounts, or allowances that may be incurred or allowed in the collection of the receivables.

(Continued)

Page Two

Inventories:
The Company's inventory in the amount of $ ___________ as determined by actual count by competent employees under the supervision of management as of December 31, 2003 are fairly stated on the first-in, first-out, lower-of-cost-or-market basis. Reasonable allowance has been made for slow-moving, obsolete, unsaleable, or unusable items. All inventories are the property of the Company. Inventory balances do not include (1) amounts of goods consigned to the Company, (2) merchandise billed to customers on or before the inventory date, or (3) any items for which the liability has not been provided on the books.

Property, Plant, and Equipment:
Property, plant and equipment is owned with satisfactory title. Capitalizable charges and purchased additions during the year are stated at cost. Property disposed of or abandoned was removed from the accounts. The provision for depreciation in the amount of $______________was determined on a basis consistent with preceding years. In our opinion, depreciation methods used and depreciable lives assigned are appropriate for allocating the cost of the assets over their useful lives. The valuation account, accumulated depreciation (balance of $___________) , is reasonably adequate to state property, plant, and equipment assets at a reasonable book value with respect to the utilization expected over their remaining lives.

All significant mortgages, assignments, pledges, or other encumbrances of assets have been disclosed to you.

Other Assets:
The Company had satisfactory title to all other assets at December 31, 2003. Any assets pledged as security for liabilities have been disclosed to you.

Liabilities:
With the possible exception of a few minor amounts, all direct liabilities of the Company amount to $______________and were recorded on the books as of December 31, 2003.

(Continued)

Page Three

The Company had no contingent or other possible liabilities which have not been disclosed to you.

Purchase and Sales Commitments:
At December 31, 2003, the Company had no important unfilled contracts for purchases in excess of normal requirements or at prices substantially in excess of market, or for sales at prices that are expected to result in a loss.

Capital Stock:
All capital stock issued or reserved for options, warrants, or other future issuance is disclosed in the financial statements.

Minutes:
Minutes of meetings of stockholders and directors as exhibited to you are complete and authentic records of all such meetings held during the period from January 1, 2003 through December 31, 2003.

General:
No events have occurred and no facts have been discovered since December 31, 2003, which would make the balance sheet at that date or the statement of earnings for the year then ended materially inaccurate or misleading. No shortages or irregularities have been discovered that have not been disclosed to you and to our knowledge there is nothing reflecting upon the honesty of members of our organization.

No charges are pending against the Company for alleged violations of federal, state, or local laws, which would have any material effect on the financial statements.

No director, officer, or principal holder of the Company's equity securities was indebted (except for minor amounts for ordinary travel and expenses) to the Company at any time during the year.

Very truly yours,

Lawrence Lancaster

President
Apple Blossom Cologne Company

Parker Shelton

Controller
Apple Blossom Cologne Company

Apple Blossom Cologne Company G-7

Contingent Liabilities and Subsequent Events

December 31, 2003

Apple Blossom Cologne Company
Unrecorded Liability Search
December 31, 2003

G-8

IV
Current Year's Working Trial Balance

Apple Blossom Cologne Company TB-BS

Working Trial Balance–Balance Sheet

12-31-03

		Working Paper Reference	Per Audit 12-31-02	Per Books 12-31-03	Adjustments Debit	Adjustments Credit	Per Audit 12-31-03	Reclassification Items Debit	Reclassification Items Credit	Financial Statements 12-31-03
Assets:										
101	Cash–Big City National Bank		513,617	846,541						
102	Cash–Second National Bank		5,918	36,968						
103	Petty cash		420	500						
105	Accounts receivable		139,504	212,705						
106	Allowance for bad debts		(11,889)	(19,919)						
107	Miscellaneous receivables									
109	Inventory		873,766	719,647						
110	Prepaid insurance		35,336	38,636						
111	Prepaid rent		5,000	1,250						
112	Office supplies inventory		8,657	9,964						
113	Small tools inventory		7,162	6,541						
115	Investment in Securities		474,518	223,033						
116	Allow. for unreal. gain/loss		6,473	6,473						
201	Long-term investments									
210	Land		82,250	82,250						
220	Buildings		276,263	276,263						
221	Accum. depn. – buildings		(65,416)	(74,625)						
230	Machinery and equipment		540,845	1,006,045						
231	Accum. depn. – mach. & equip.		(160,866)	(189,848)						
240	Automotive equipment		99,425	99,425						
241	Accum. depn. – auto. equip.		(52,798)	(77,654)						
250	Office furniture & fixtures		106,433	114,833						
251	Accum. depn. – off. furn. & fix.		(37,581)	(43,113)						
	Total assets		2,847,037	3,275,915						
Liabilities:										
301	Accounts payable		223,161	135,550						
302	Accrued Payroll Taxes		113,846	86,253						
303	Wages and Salaries Payable		81,239							
304	Accrued Property Taxes		14,113	21,988						
305	Accrued interest		10,625	15,833						
306	Dividends payable		17,575	23,125						
307	Federal income tax payable		63,772	25,000						
308	Notes payable–short term		125,000							
350	Lease obligation – short-term									
401	Notes payable–long term			475,000						
450	Lease obligation – long-term									
	Total liabilities		649,331	782,749						

Apple Blossom Cologne Company TB–BS

Working Trial Balance–Balance Sheet

12-31-03

		Working Paper Reference	Per Audit 12-31-02	Per Books 12-31-03	Adjustments Debit	Adjustments Credit	Per Audit 12-31-03	Reclassification Items Debit	Reclassification Items Credit	Financial Statements 12-31-03
Owners' Equity:										
501	Common stock		925,000	925,000						
505	Other contributed capital		736,550	736,550						
506	Unrea Gain/Loss Investments		6,473	6,473						
601	Retained earnings		272,435	529,683						
605	Dividends		(17,575)	(23,125)						
610	Current net income		274,823	318,585						
	Total owners' equity		2,197,706	2,493,166						
	Total liabilities & owners' equity		2,847,037	3,275,915						

Apple Blossom Cologne Company — TB-IS

Working Trial Balance – Income Statement

12-31-03

Acct.	Account	Working Paper Reference	Per Audit 12-31-02	Per Books 12-31-03	Adjustments Debit	Adjustments Credit	Per Audit 12-31-03	Reclassificati Items Debit
REVENUE:								
701	Sales		3,906,577	4,272,623				
703	Sales Returns & Allowances		(29,820)	(33,051)				
	Net Sales		3,876,757	4,239,572				
EXPENSES:								
801	Cost of Goods Sold		1,596,800	1,742,503				
	Gross Margin		2,279,957	2,497,069				
OPERATING EXPENSES:								
820	Wage and Salary Expense		1,528,700	1,618,643				
821	Payroll Tax Expense		129,959	128,033				
822	Depreciation Expense		64,422	80,459				
823	Rent Expense		3,750	3,750				
824	Office Supplies Expense		9,683	12,380				
825	Small Tools Expense		3,359	6,419				
826	Advertising Expense		12,714	44,934				
827	Insurance		28,930	32,765				
828	Repairs and Maintenance		17,869	14,240				
829	Property Tax		14,113	21,988				
830	Utilities		11,742	14,760				
831	Professional Fees		13,347	37,140				
832	Miscellaneous Expense		494	825				
833	Provision for Bad Debts		11,156	22,790				
834	Freight Expense		31,641	46,310				
	Total Operating Expenses		1,881,879	2,085,436				
	Net Income From Operations		398,078	411,633				
OTHER INCOME (EXPENSE):								
901	Interest Expense		(27,500)	(21,146)				
910	Gain(Loss)Sale of Investments			25,975				
920	Income From Investments		9,379	7,393				
930	Gain(Loss)Sale of Fixed Assets		18,638	(15,270)				
950	Miscellaneous Income			10,000				
	Net Other Income		517	6,952				
	Net Income Before Taxes		398,595	418,585				
940	Federal Income Tax		123,772	100,000				
	Net Income		274,823	318,585				

	Financial
	Statements
Credit	12-31-03

Apple Blossom Cologne Company AJE

Proposed Adjusting Journal Entries

12-31-03

	ACCOUNT DESCRIPTION		ACCOUNT NUMBER	DEBIT	CREDIT

V
Prior Year's Working Papers

APPLE BLOSSOM COLOGNE COMPANY
Senior's Audit Memorandum
December 31, 2002

To: Partner-in-Charge
Apple Blossom Cologne Company Audit

As senior-in-charge of the audit examination of the financial statements of Apple Blossom Cologne Company for the year ended December 31, 2002, I have prepared all accompanying working papers in accordance with generally accepted auditing standards and included all procedures considered necessary in the circumstances. I have performed all steps of the audit program. Other than those described in the following paragraphs, there were no special accounting or auditing problems encountered.

When searching for unrecorded liabilities, it was discovered that the Company had not recorded a December utility invoice. I proposed an adjusting entry to record the $2,025 liability. Moreover, the Company had incorrectly extended inventory, for which I proposed a $2,650 adjustment.

The Company is liable to Big City National Bank for an unsecured note in the amount of $125,000. The note, which is due April 30, 2003, has been disclosed in the footnotes. No contingent liabilities were observed.

It is my opinion that the accompanying draft of the client's financial statements is in accordance with generally accepted accounting principles with proper disclosure and that we may issue the unqualified opinion as shown in the accompanying draft of the audit report.

Jasper W. Parsons
Audit Senior
February 7, 2003

ANDERSON, OLDS, & WATERSHED

Certified Public Accountants
615 Big City National Bank Building
Main at Michigan Avenue
Chicago, Illinois 60612
Phone: (312) 555-4452
Fax: (312) 555-9991
www.aowcpa.com

INDEPENDENT AUDITOR□S REPORT

Board of Directors and Stockholders
The Apple Blossom Cologne Company

We have audited the accompanying balance sheets of Apple Blossom Cologne Company, Inc. as of December 31, 2002 and 2001, and the related statements of income, changes in stockholders□ equity, and cash flows for the years then ended. These financial statements are the responsibility of the Company's management. Our responsibility is to express an opinion on these financial statements based on our audits.

We conducted our audits in accordance with generally accepted auditing standards. Those standards require that we plan and perform the audit to obtain reasonable assurance about whether the financial statements are free of material misstatement. An audit includes examining, on a test basis, evidence supporting the amounts and disclosures in the financial statements. An audit also includes assessing the accounting principles used and significant estimates made by management, as well as evaluating the overall financial statement presentation. We believe that our audits provide a reasonable basis for our opinion.

In our opinion, the financial statements referred to above present fairly, in all material respects, the financial position of Apple Blossom Cologne Company as of December 31, 2002 and 2001, and the results of its operations and its cash flows for the years then ended in conformity with generally accepted accounting principles.

Anderson, Olds, and Watershed
Certified Public Accountants
February 7, 2003

APPLE BLOSSOM COLOGNE COMPANY
Balance Sheet
December 31, 2002 and 2001

ASSETS

	2002	*2001*
Current Assets:		
Cash	$519,955	$368,606
Accounts receivable less allowance for losses 2002, $11,889; 2001, $13,769	127,615	130,244
Inventories (Note 1)	873,766	588,139
Prepaid expenses	56,155	60,204
Investment in securities (Notes 1 and 2)	480,991	331,694
Total Current Assets	2,058,482	1,478,887
Property, plant, & equipment, at cost (Note 1):		
Land	82,250	103,250
Buildings	276,263	243,250
Machinery and equipment	540,845	535,800
Automotive equipment	99,425	90,125
Office furniture and fixtures	106,433	99,775
	1,105,216	1,072,200
Less accumulated depreciation	316,661	252,239
	788,555	819,961
TOTAL ASSETS	$2,847,037	$2,298,848
LIABILITIES AND STOCKHOLDERS' EQUITY		
Current Liabilities:		
Accounts payable	$223,161	$140,649
Accrued liabilities	219,823	191,613
Notes payable (Note 3)	125,000	
Dividends payable	17,575	13,875
Income taxes payable (Note 4)	63,772	14,230
Total current liabilities	649,331	360,367
Total Liabilities	649,331	360,367
Stockholders' Equity:		
Common stock, par value $100, authorized 20,000 shares, issued and outstanding 9,250 shares	925,000	925,000
Contributed capital in excess of par value	736,550	736,550
Unrealized gain<loss>on investments	6,473	4,496
Retained earnings	529,683	272,435
Total Stockholders' Equity	2,197,706	1,938,481
TOTAL LIABILITIES AND STOCKHOLDERS' EQUITY	$2,847,037	$2,298,848

APPLE BLOSSOM COLOGNE COMPANY
Statement of Income
Years Ended December 31, 2002 and 2001

	2002	*2001*
Net sales and other revenues	$3,876,757	$3,333,272
Cost of goods sold	1,596,800	1,352,291
Gross margin	2,279,957	1,980,981
Operating expenses:		
Selling, general, and administrative (Note 5)	1,817,457	1,733,694
Depreciation (Note 1)	64,422	60,778
	1,881,879	1,794,472
Operating Income	398,078	186,509
Other income (expense) and adjustments:		
Interest	(27,500)	(25,290)
Other income	9,379	24,760
Gain on sale of fixed assets	18,638	13,893
Net income before federal income taxes	398,595	199,872
Provision for income taxes (Notes 1 and 4)	123,772	56,206
NET INCOME	$274,823	$143,666
Earnings per common share (Note 6)	$29.71	$15.53

APPLE BLOSSOM COLOGNE COMPANY
Statement of Changes in Stockholders' Equity
Years Ended December 31, 2002 and 2001

	2002	*2001*
Common Stock:		
Common stock at beginning of year	$925,000	$925,000
Common stock at end of year	$925,000	$925,000
Contributed capital:		
Contributed capital at beginning of year	$736,550	$736,550
Contributed capital at end of year	$736,550	$736,550
Unrealized Gain<Loss>on Investments:		
Unrealized Gain<Loss>at beginning of year	$4,496	$4,128
Change in unrealized gain<loss>	1,977	368
Unrealized Gain<Loss>at end of year	$6,473	$4,496
Retained Earnings:		
Retained earnings at beginning of year	$272,435	$142,644
Net income for the year	274,823	143,666
Dividends	(17,575)	(13,875)
Retained earnings at end of year	$529,683	$272,435

APPLE BLOSSOM COLOGNE COMPANY
Statement of Cash Flows
Years Ended December 31, 2002 and 2001

	2002	*2001*
Cash flows from operating activities:		
Net income	$274,823	$143,666
Add <Deduct> items not using <providing> cash:		
Depreciation	64,422	60,778
Change in accounts receivable	4,509	(23,981)
Change in allowance for bad debts	(1,880)	(5,693)
Change in inventory	(285,627)	(52,480)
Change in prepaid expenses	4,049	(8,740)
Change in accounts payable	82,512	25,281
Change in accrued liabilities	28,210	(57,549)
Change in income taxes payable	49,542	(4,214)
Gain or loss--sale of assets	(18,638)	(13,893)
Gain or loss--sale of investments		(13,874)
Net cash provided--operating activities	$201,922	$49,301
Cash flows from investing activities:		
Cash provided		
Sale of assets	39,638	52,664
Cash disbursed		
Purchase of assets	54,016	74,900
Purchase of securities	147,320	
Net cash provided <used>--investing activities	($161,698)	($22,236)
Cash flows from financing activities:		
Cash provided		
Issuance of notes payable	245,000	250,000
Cash disbursed		
Dividends paid	13,875	12,500
Payments on notes	120,000	250,000
Net cash provided <used>--financing activities	$111,125	($12,500)
Net increase <decrease> in cash	151,349	14,565
Cash at beginning of year	368,606	354,041
Cash at end of year	$519,955	$368,606

Supplemental Disclosures of Cash Flow Information

	2002	*2001*
Interest paid	$16,875	$14,995
Income taxes paid	74,230	51,996

APPLE BLOSSOM COLOGNE COMPANY
Notes to Financial Statements

Note 1--Summary of Significant Accounting Policies

The accounting policies employed by the Apple Blossom Cologne Company are in accordance with generally accepted accounting principles. In those instances where more than one generally accepted accounting principle can be applied, the company has adopted the one it believes most accurately and fairly reflects the situation, as described in the following paragraphs.

Investments in Securities--Equity securities are classified as available-for-sale. Debt securities are classified as either available-for-sale or held-to-maturity, depending upon the intent of management. Investments in the available-for-sale portfolio are carried at fair value, normally obtainable from quotations available on securities exchanges. Debt securities in the held-to-maturity portfolio are carried at amortized cost. Premium or discount is amortized using the effective interest method. Unrealized holding gains and losses due to the difference between cost and fair value are included in stockholders' equity. In computing gains and losses, the specific identification method is used to determine cost.

Inventories--Inventories are stated at the lower-of-cost-or-market. Cost is determined by the first-in, first-out method. Market value is considered to be the current sales price less distribution cost for finished products and replacement cost for other inventories. Physical inventories are taken each year at year-end.

Property, plant, and equipment--Fixed assets are stated at cost. Repair and maintenance, rearrangement costs, and renewals and betterments which do not increase the basic productive capacity of the assets are charged to cost and expensed as incurred. When fixed assets are disposed of, the cost and related accumulated depreciation are removed from the accounts and any resulting gain or loss is reflected in income. Depreciation is provided on groups of assets in the year of acquisition and disposal using the straight-line method..

Definition of accounting year--The accounts of Apple Blossom Cologne Company are on a calendar year basis.

Income taxes--When timing differences between financial and tax reporting occur, deferred income taxes are provided.

Note 2--Investments in Securities

At December 31, 2002, the company held investments in equity securities, included in current assets, having an aggregate fair value of $480,991 and a cost of $474,518. The net unrealized holding gain at December 31, 2002 was $6,473; this amount was included in a separate component of stockholders' equity. The net unrealized holding gain of $6,473 is composed of gross unrealized holding gains of $25,400 and gross unrealized holding losses of $18,927. The change in net unrealized holding gain or loss from December 31, 2001 amounted to $1,977. At December 31, 2001, investments in equity securities included in current assets had an aggregate fair value of $331,694 and a cost of $327,198. The net unrealized holding gain at December 31, 2001 was $4,496, composed of gross unrealized holding gains of $4,496 and no unrealized holding losses. The change in net unrealized holding gain or loss from December 31, 2000 amounted to $1,275.

Note 3--Long-term and Short-term Debt

Debt outstanding at December 31, 2002, consisted of a $125,000 note to Big City National Bank dated April 30, 2002, due April 30, 2003, unsecured, 12 3/4% interest payable April 30, 2003. There was no debt outstanding at December 31, 2001.

Note 4--Income Taxes

Income Taxes were calculated on 2002 before-tax income of $398,595 and 2001 before-tax net income of $199,872. Applicable tax amounts were $123,772 for 2002 and $56,206 for 2001. Income taxes payable at December 31, 2002 and 2001 were $63,772 and $14,230, respectively.

Note 5--Lease Commitment

The company leases a warehouse under an operating lease agreement executed on May 1, 2000. The total rental expense amounted to $3,750 per year for both 2002 and 2001. At December 31, 2002, the ten-year operating lease had a remaining term of seven years four months with a biennial rent commitment of $7,500, paid in advance on May 1 of each even-numbered year. The total remaining rent commitment at December 31, 2002 was $22,500 and $30,000 at December 31, 2001.

Note 6--Earnings Per Share

Primary earnings per share are computed by dividing net income by the weighted average number of shares of common stock outstanding during each year. There were no common stock equivalents. Therefore, fully diluted earnings per share are the same as primary earnings per share.

Apple Blossom Cologne Company — TB-BS

Working Trial Balance—Balance Sheet — 1-31-03

12-31-02 — JWP

Acct.	Account	Working Paper Reference	Per Audit 12-31-01	Per Books 12-31-02	Adjustments Debit		Adjustments Credit		Per Audit 12-31-02	Reclassification Items Debit	Reclassification Items Credit	Financial Statements 12-31-02
Assets:												
101	Cash—Big City National Bank	A-1	323,736	513,692			75	(2	513,617			
102	Cash—Second National Bank	A-3	44,370	5,918					5,918			519,955
103	Petty Cash	A-6	500	500			80	(3	420			
105	Accounts receivable	B-1	144,013	140,344			840	(1	139,504			127,615
106	Allowance for bad debts	B-5	(13,769)	(12,729)	840	(1)			(11,889)			
109	Inventory	C-1	588,139	876,416			2,650	(4	873,766			873,766
110	Prepaid Insurance	D-1	50,538	35,336					35,336			
111	Prepaid Rent	D-3	1,250	5,000					5,000			56,155
112	Office Supplies Inventory	D-3	5,071	8,657					8,657			
113	Small Tools Inventory	D-3	3,345	7,162					7,162			
115	Investment in Securities	E-1	327,198	474,518					474,518			480,991
116	Allow. for Unreal. Gain/loss	E-1	4,496	4,496	1,977	(7)			6,473			
210	Land	F-1	103,250	82,250					82,250			82,250
220	Buildings	F-1	243,250	276,263					276,263			276,263
221	Accum. depn. — buildings	F-1	(56,758)	(65,416)					(65,416)			
230	Machinery and equipment	F-1	535,800	540,845					540,845			540,845
231	Accum. depn. — mach. & equip.	F-1	(133,950)	(160,866)					(160,866)			
240	Automotive equipment	F-1	90,125	99,425					99,425			99,425
241	Accum. depn. — auto. equip.	F-1	(29,105)	(52,798)					(52,798)			
250	Office furniture & fixtures	F-1	99,775	106,433					106,433			106,433
251	Accum. depn. — off. furn. & fix.	F-1	(32,426)	(37,581)					(37,581)	Total accum. depn.		(316,661)
	Total assets		2,298,848	2,847,865					2,847,037			2,847,037
Liabilities:												
301	Accounts payable	G-1	140,649	221,136			2,025	(5	223,161			223,161
302	Accrued Payroll Taxes	H-1	104,936	77,191			36,655	(6	113,846			
303	Wages and Salaries Payable	H-2	77,177				81,239	(6	81,239			219,523
304	Accrued Property Taxes	H-3	9,500	14,113					14,113			
305	Accrued interest	I-1		10,625					10,625			
306	Dividends payable	H-3	13,875	17,575					17,575			17,575
307	Federal income tax payable	H-4	14,230	20,000			43,772	(8	63,772			63,772
308	Notes payable—short term	I-1		125,000					125,000			125,000
	Total liabilities		360,367	485,640					649,331			649,331
Owners' Equity:												
501	Common stock	J-1	925,000	925,000					925,000			925,000
505	Other contributed capital	J-1	736,550	736,550					736,550			736,550
506	Unrea Gain/Loss Investments	E-1	4,496	4,496			1,977	(7	6,473			6,473
601	Retained earnings	K-1	142,644	272,435					272,435			
605	Dividends	K-1,H-3	(13,875)	(17,575)					(17,575)			529,683
610	Current net income	TB-IS	143,666	441,319	166,496				274,823			
	Total owners' equity		1,938,481	2,362,225					2,197,706			2,197,706
	Total liabilities & owners' equity		2,298,848	2,847,865	169,313		169,313		2,847,037			2,847,037

Apple Blossom Cologne Company | TB-IS
Working Trial Balance-Income Statement | 1-31-03
12-31-02 | JWP

		Working Paper Reference	Per Audit 12-31-01	Per Books 12-31-02	Adjustments Debit		Adjustments Credit	Per Audit 12-31-02	Reclassification Items Debit	Reclassification Items Credit	Financial Statements 12-31-02
REVENUE:											
701	Sales		3,388,364	3,906,577				3,906,577			3,906,577
703	Sales Returns & Allowances		(55,092)	(29,820)				(29,820)			(29,820)
	Net Sales		3,333,272	3,876,757				3,876,757			3,876,757
EXPENSES:											
801	Cost of Goods Sold		1,352,291	1,594,150	2,650	(4)		1,596,800			1,596,800
	Gross Margin		1,980,981	2,282,607				2,279,957			2,279,957
OPERATING EXPENSES:											
820	Wage and Salary Expense	H-1	1,452,250	1,423,672	105,028	(6)		1,528,700			1,528,700
821	Payroll Tax Expense	H-1	119,560	117,093	12,866	(6)		129,959			129,959
822	Depreciation Expense	F-1	60,778	64,422				64,422			64,422
823	Rent Expense	D-3	3,750	3,750				3,750			3,750
824	Office Supplies Expense	D-3	8,211	9,683				9,683			9,683
825	Small Tools Expense	D-3	2,655	3,359				3,359			3,359
826	Advertising Expense		14,196	12,714				12,714			12,714
827	Insurance	D-1	25,768	28,930				28,930			28,930
828	Repairs and Maintenance	F-5	12,024	17,869				17,869			17,869
829	Property Tax	H-3	14,793	14,113				14,113			14,113
830	Utilities		11,523	9,717	2,025	(5)		11,742			11,742
831	Professional Fees		12,645	13,347				13,347			13,347
832	Miscellaneous Expense		6,872	339	155	(2,3)		494			494
833	Provision for Bad Debts	B-5	11,521	11,156				11,156			11,156
834	Freight Expense		37,926	31,641				31,641			31,641
	Total Operating Expenses		1,794,472	1,761,805				1,881,879			1,881,879
	Net Income From Operations		186,509	520,802				398,078			398,078
OTHER INCOME (EXPENSE):											
901	Interest Expense	I-1	(25,290)	(27,500)				(27,500)			(27,500)
910	Gain(Loss)Sale of Investments	E-3	13,874					-			-
920	Income From Investments		8,582	9,379				9,379			9,379
930	Gain(Loss)Sale of Fixed Assets	F-3	13,893	18,638				18,638			18,638
950	Miscellaneous Income		2,304	-				-			-
	Net Other Income		13,363	517				517			517
	Net Income Before Taxes		199,872	521,319				398,595			398,595
940	Federal Income Tax	H-4	56,206	80,000	43,772	(8)		123,772			123,772
	Net Income		143,666	441,319	166,496			274,823			274,823

Apple Blossom Cologne Company — AJE

Proposed Adjusting Journal Entries — 2-3-03

December 31, 2002 — JWP

Account Description	Account Number	Debit	Credit
(AJE # 1)			
Allowance for bad debts	106	840	
Accounts receivable	105		840
To write off uncollectible accounts per (B-1).			
(AJE # 2)			
Miscellaneous expense	832	75	
Cash	101		75
To record bank service charges per (A-1).			
(AJE # 3)			
Miscellaneous expense	832	80	
Petty cash fund	103		80
To record unreimbursed vouchers in petty cash per (A-6).			
(AJE # 4)			
Cost of goods sold	801	2650	
Inventory	109		2650
To correct inventory extension error per (C-1).			
(AJE # 5)			
Utilities expense	830	2025	
Accounts payable	301		2025
To record unrecorded liability per (G-2).			
(AJE # 6)			
Wage & salary expense	820	105028	
Payroll tax expense	821	12866	
Accrued payroll taxes	302		36655
Wages & salaries payable	303		81239
To record accrued wages and salaries per (H-2)			
(AJE # 7)			
Allowance for unreal. gain/loss	116	1977	
Unreal. gain/loss on investments	506		1977
To record unrealized holding gain on securities per (E-1).			
(AJE # 8)			
Federal income tax expense	940	43772	
Federal income taxes payable	307		43772
To adjust federal income taxes per (H-4).			

Apple Blossom Cologne Company	RJE
Proposed Adjusting Journal Entries	2-3-03
December 31, 2002	JWP

	Account Description			Account Number	Debit	Credit
	None required					

ANDERSON, OLDS, & WATERSHED

Certified Public Accountants
615 Big City National Bank Building
Main at Michigan Avenue
Chicago, Illinois 60612
Phone: (312) 555-4452
Fax: (312) 555-9991
Internet: www.aowcpa.com

February 7, 2003

The Board of Directors of Apple Blossom Cologne Company:

In planning and performing our audit of the financial statements of the Apple Blossom Cologne Company for the year ended December 31, 2002, we considered its internal control structure in order to determine our auditing procedures for the purpose of expressing our opinion on the financial statements and not to provide assurance on the internal control structure. However, we noted certain matters involving the control structure and its operation that we consider to be reportable conditions under standards established by the American Institute of Certified Public Accountants. Reportable conditions involve matters coming to our attention relating to significant deficiencies in the design or operation of the internal control structure that, in our judgment, could adversely affect the organization's ability to record, process, summarize, and report financial data consistent with the assertions of management in the financial statements.

We have found the following deficiencies. Not all personnel within the accounting department are required to take annual vacations. Cash receipts are not deposited intact daily. Access to notes and investments is not limited to authorized personnel. Any of the foregoing deficiencies could lead to defalcations. Additionally, no specific authorization procedures exist for the purchase or sale of investments. Transactions of this type should be individually authorized by the Board of Directors.

This report is intended solely for the use of the Board of Directors, management, and others within the organization. If you would like to discuss any of these matters, we would be pleased to review them with you.

Very truly yours,

Anderson, Olds, and Watershed

Anderson, Olds, and Watershed
Certified Public Accountants

Apple Blossom Cologne Company	A-1
Bank Reconciliation—Big City National	1-21-03
12-31-02	JWP
(Prepared By Client)	

Description		Date	Detail	Total	Mark
Balance Per Bank Statement				621967	C#
Add:					
Deposit in Transit		Dec 31	16895u		
Safety deposit box charge		Dec 28	75b	16970	
Deduct:				638937	
Checks outstanding					
No.	Payee				
1063	Fruit Juicy Perfume Co.	Dec. 27	12268N		
1064	Norton Exterminators	Dec. 27	2790N		
1065	Petrozine Fuel Co.	Dec. 27	7300N		
1073	Fruit Scents, Inc.	Dec. 28	5895N		
1075	Fruit Juicy Perfume Co.	Dec. 28	11250N		
1076	Flash Freight Co.	Dec. 28	3000N		
1077	Fruit Juicy Perfume Co.	Dec. 28	32000N		
1080	Longhorn Garbage Disposa	Dec. 28	45N		
1081	Fruit Scents, Inc.	Dec. 31	8250N		
1082	Flash Freight Co.	Dec. 31	4017N		
1083	National Trucks	Dec. 31	805N		
1084	United Parcel Co.	Dec. 31	125N		
1085	Fruit Scents, Inc.	Dec. 31	37500N		
				125245	
	Balance Per Books 12-31-02			513692 ^	
Audit adjustments:				(TB-BS)	
(AJE #2)				75	
Balance per audit				513617	

^ Footed

\# Agreed to beginning balance of cutoff bank statement.

C Confirmed with bank per (A-2).

u Traced to cash receipts journal entry before year-end and to cutoff bank statment.

N Examined paid checks clearing with cutoff bank statement and traced to cash disbursements journal for Dec. 2002.

b Examined bank's debit memo dated 12-27-02. Propose (AJE #2):

Account	Description	Debit	Credit
832	Miscellaneous expense	75	
101	Cash—Big City National Bank		75

Apple Blossom Cologne Company
Bank Confirmation-Big City National
December 31, 2002

A-2
1-21-03
JWP

STANDARD FORM TO CONFIRM ACCOUNT BALANCE INFORMATION WITH FINANCIAL INSTITUTIONS

ORIGINAL

Apple Blossom Cologne Company
CUSTOMER NAME

Financial Institution's Name and Address:
[Big City National Bank
Main at Michigan Avenue
Chicago, Illinois 60612]

We have provided to our accountants the following information as of the close of business on December 31, 2002 regarding our deposit and loan balances. Please confirm the accuracy of the information, noting any exceptions to the information provided. If the balances have been left blank, please complete the form by furnishing the balance in the appropriate space below.* Although we do not request nor expect you to conduct a comprehensive, detailed search of your records, if during the process of completing this confirmation additional information about other deposit and loan accounts we may have with you comes to your attention, please include such information below. Please use the enclosed envelope to return the form directly to our accountants.

1. At the close of business on the date listed above, our records indicated the following deposit balance(s):

ACCOUNT NAME	ACCOUNT NO.	INTEREST RATE	BALANCE*
Apple Blossom Cologne Company General Account	146-2013	N/A	$621,967 (A-1)

2. We were directly liable to the financial institution for loans at the close of business on the date listed above as follows:

ACCOUNT NO./ DESCRIPTION	BALANCE*	DATE DUE	INTEREST RATE	DATE THROUGH WHICH INTEREST IS PAID	DESCRIPTION OF COLLATERAL
A/C# 013756	$125,000	4-30-03	12-3/4%	interest is paid through 4-30-02	Unsecured

Lillian Stockton
(Customer's Authorized Signature)

January 2, 2003
(Date)

The information presented above by the customer is in agreement with our records. Although we have not conducted a comprehensive, detailed search of our records, no other deposit or loan accounts have come to our attention except as noted below.

Buford Churchill
(Financial Institution Authorized Signature)

January 7, 2003
(Date)

Cashier
(Title)

EXCEPTIONS AND/OR COMMENTS

Please return this form directly to our accountants:
[Anderson, Olds, and Watershed
Certified Public Accountants
615 Big City Bank Building
Chicago, Illinois 60612]

* Ordinarily, balances are intentionally left blank if they are not available at the time the form is prepared.

Approved 1990 by American Bankers Association, American Institute of Certified Public Accountants, and Bank Administration Institute. Additional forms available from: AICPA–Order Department, P.O. Box 2209, Jersey City, NJ 07303-2209

D451 5951

Apple Blossom Cologne Company — A-3

Bank Reconciliation—Second National (payroll) — 1-21-03

12-31-02 — JWP

(Prepared By Client)

Balance Per Bank Statement				7453 C#
Deduct:				
Checks outstanding				
No.	Payee			
5997	Bert Campo	Dec. 27	297N	
5998	Patricia Sanders	Dec. 27	312N	
5999	Raymond Arthur	Dec. 27	262N	
6000	David Johnson	Dec. 27	346N	
6001	Elizabeth Robertson	Dec. 27	318N	1535
	Balance Per Books 12-31-02			5918 ^
Audit adjustments:				(TB-BS)
None				
Balance per audit				5918

^ Footed

Agreed to beginning balance of cutoff bank statement.

C Confirmed with bank per (A-4).

N Examined paid checks clearing with cutoff bank statement and traced to cash disbursements journal for Dec. 2002.

Apple Blossom Cologne Company — A-6

Petty Cash — 1-21-03

12-31-02 — JWP

	Denomination		Number	Amount	Total	
Currency		10	20	200		
		5	29	145		
		1	41	41	386	
Coins	Halves		12	6		
	Quarters		36	9		
	Dimes		30	3		
	Nickels		200	10		
	Pennies		600	6	34	
Checks			none	0	0	
Total cash					420	
Petty Cash Vouchers						
(1) U.S. Post Office—stamps				Dec. 28	80	n
Petty cash per client					500	
					(TB-BS)	
Audit adjustments						
(AJE #3)					80	
Balance per audit					420	

The above fund was examined in my presence and returned to me intact on this date, 12-31-02, 4:30pm.

Pam Lewis
Cashier

n Propose (AJE #3) for reimbursed vouchers on 12-31-02:

Miscellaneous expense	832	80	
Petty cash	103		80

Apple Blossom Cologne Company — B-1

Accounts Receivable – Aged Trial Balance — 1-24-03

12-31-02 — JWP

(Prepared by Client)

	Customer	Current 1-30 days	30-60 Days	60-90 Days	Over 90 Days	Total		Confirmation Mailed 1-3-03	Subsequent Collection to 1-14-03	Comments by Credit Manager–B. Robertson
	All-Right Discount Drugs		3382@			3382@		negative	---	Sometimes slow. Good account.
	Bobell Beauty Supplies			4943@		4943@		negative	2943R	Slow paying.
	Body Bar	4500@	500@	645@		5645@		negative	2645R	Slow paying, but always does.
	Cut-Rate Discount Stores	2450@	3050@	250@		5750@		negative	1250R	Slow paying. Good account.
	Darings	3125@				3125@		negative	1900R	
	Frankies Floral Frag.	5500@	5000@			10500@	C(B-2)	positive	---	Good Account.
	Kanine Kaffiures				840@	840@	#(B-3)	positive	---	Company out of business.
	Lone Star Supply	5002@				5002@		negative	1500R	
	Rausch's Dept.Store	3733@	875@			4608@		negative	2125R	Good Account.
	Tears & Doefall Comp.	44800@	6200@	5250@		56250@	C(B-3)	positive	43000R	Sometimes slow--good account.
	William's Fragrances	9700@	2050@			11750@	C(B-4)	positive	9000R	Good Account.
	Young & Beautiful	11250@				11250@	C(B-4)	positive	11250R	
	Various Other Acct's.	14299@		3000@		17299@			---	Some slow, but all good accounts.
	Per client	104359	21057	14088	840	140344			75613	
		^	^	^	^	^^				
	Audit adjustments					(TB-BS)				
	(AJE # 1)				(840)	(840)				
	Per audit	104359	21057	14088	–	139504				

Percentage of accounts receivable collected as of 1/14/03:

$75613/139504 = 54%

^ Footed.

^^ Footed and crossfooted.

@ Balances and aging traced from subsidiary ledger.

C Positive confirmation mailed. No exceptions noted.

Confirmation sent; returned by post office unopened. Propose (AJE #1) to write off receivable:

		Dr.	Cr.
106	Allowance for bad debts	840	
105	Accounts receivable		840

R Corresponds with entry in cash receipts journal.

Note: No negative confimations were returned.

Apple Blossom Cologne Company — B-4
Receivables Confirmation — 1-22-03
December 31, 2002 — JWP

CONFIRMATION OF ACCOUNTS RECEIVABLE

Confirmation Request No. 4

Anderson, Olds, and Watershed
Certified Public Accountants
615 Big City National Bank Building
Main at Michigan Avenue
Chicago, Illinois 60612

Dear Sir or Madam:

The statement of our account showing a balance of $ 11,750 (1) (B-1) as of 12/31/02 is correct except as noted below.

Very truly yours,
William's Fragrances
William Brown

Date January 20, 2003

Exceptions:
No exceptions
(1) Traced $9,000 of this amount to January collection recorded in cash receipts journal per (B-1). JWP

CONFIRMATION OF ACCOUNTS RECEIVABLE

Confirmation Request No. 5

Anderson, Olds, and Watershed
Certified Public Accountants
615 Big City National Bank Building
Main at Michigan Avenue
Chicago, Illinois 60612

Dear Sir or Madam:

The statement of our account showing a balance of $ 11,250 (1) (B-1) as of 12/31/02 is correct except as noted below.

Very truly yours,
Young and Beautiful
Roger McAdams
President

Date January 17, 2003

Exceptions:
None.
(1) Traced $11,250 to January collection recorded in cash receipts journal per (B-1) JWP.

Apple Blossom Cologne Company — B-5

Allowance for Bad Debts — 1-22-03

12-31-02 — JWP

			Allowance for Bad Debts		Provision for Bad Debts
Balance at 12-31-01			13769	A	
2002 write-offs			12195	Y	
			1574		
2002 provision			11156	Z	11156
Balance per client at 12-31-02			12729		11156
			(TB-BS)		(TB-IS)
Adjusting journal entries:					
(AJE # 2) (B-1)			(840)		
Adjusted balance			11889	(2) n	11156
Journal entry to adjust allowance account:					
(None required)					
Balance per audit			11889		11156

Provision For Bad Debts Reasonableness Test:

AGE	AGED AMOUNT		EXPECTED UNCOLL. PERCENT	EST UNCOLL.	
1-30	104359	(B-1)	1.50%	1565	
30-60	21057	(B-1)	10.00%	2106	
60-90	14088	(B-1)	50.00%	7044	
Over 90	0	(1)	100.00%	0	
Balance per Analysis				10715	
Adjusted Balance				11889	(2) n
Difference				1174	

A Agreed to prior year's working papers.

Y All write-offs approved by credit manager.

Z Provision appears reasonable and in line with prior years.

n Allowance balance per reasonableness test is lower than client balance per books. Client declined to reduce the account. The adjusted balance appears reasonable and is in line with prior year. As the adjustment would increase income and is less than 1% of net income (before adjustments), no adjustment is considered necessary. JWP

(1) \$840 - \$840 = 0
(B-1) (AJE #2)

Apple Blossom Cologne Company — C-1

Inventory — 1-21-03

12-31-02 — JWP

Item	Size Ounces	Number of Cases	Number of Bottles (24/Case)	Total Ounces	Cost per Unit	Amount Inventory	Totals		Notes
Oils									
#A601 Lemon	2	372.00	8928	17856N	2.50/oz<	44640Y			
#A603 Lemon	4	146.00	3504	14016N	2.50/oz<	35040Y			
#A608 Lemon	6	104.00	2496	14976N	2.50/oz<	37440Y			
#R315 Apple	4	114.00	2736	10944N	2.25/oz<	24624Y			
#R320 Apple	6	25.00	600	3600N	2.25/oz<	8100Y			
#Q291 Magnolia	8	231.00	5544	44352N	2.11/oz<	93583Y			
Total Oils:							243427		Note:
Cremes									Current cost obtained and found to
#H84 Hand Creme	4	613.33	14720N	---	4.00/oz<	58880Y			exceed inventory carrying value.
#F60 Face Creme	4	580.00	13920N	---	4.25/oz<	59160Y			No lower of cost or market adjustment
Total Cremes							118040		necessa JWP
Lotions									
#L612 Moisturizing	8	740.00	17760N	---	3.00/oz<	53280Y			
#L940 Skin Tone	8	758.00	18192N	---	2.86/oz<	54679Y		^	Footed
#L818 Smoothing	8	784.00	18816N	---	2.73/oz<	51368Y		Y	Extensions recalculated.
Total Lotions							159327	N	Quantities traced from inventory observation.
Colognes								<	FIFO costing vouched to vendor invoice (freight and
#E801 L'Eau de Pomme	8	190.00	4560	36480N	2.80/oz<	102144Y			discounts included where applicable).
#E802 L'Eau de Abricot	8	97.50	2340	18720N	2.80/oz<	52416Y		X	Client error in extending--should be $52,029.
#E803 L'Eau de Teint	8	109.00	2616	20928N	2.80/oz<	58598Y			Propose (AJE #3) to correct:
#E804 L'Eau de Chevrefeue	8	50.00	1200	9600N	2.80/oz<	26880Y			801 Cost of goods sold 2650
#E805 L'Eau de Jasmin	8	42.50	1020	8160N	2.80/oz<	22848Y			109 Inventory 2650
#E806 L'Eau de Citron	8	62.50	1500	12000N	2.80/oz<	33600Y			
#E807 L'Eau de Rose	8	110.00	2640	21120N	2.80/oz<	59136Y			
Total Colognes							355622		
Per client 12-31-02		5128 5/6	123092	------	------	------	876416		
		^	^				^		
							(TB-BS)		
					Audit adjustments:				
					(AJE # 4)		(2650)		
					Per audit		873766		

Apple Blossom Cologne Company						C−2				
Inventory Observation and Test Counts						1−1−03				
December 31, 2002						JWP				
Stock Number	**Item**	**Number of Cases**	**Number of Bottles (24/Case)**	**Size of Bottle**	**Total Ounces**					
STOREROOM:			C							
L818	Smoothing Lotion	704n	16896*	8 oz	135168					
L612	Moisturizing Lotion	740	17760*	8 oz	142080					
L940	Skin Tone Lotion	758n	18192*	8 oz	145536					
F60	Face Creme	580	13920*	4 oz	55680					
H84	Hand Creme	493 1/3n	11840*	4 oz	47360					
E804	L'Eau de Chevrefeuelle	50n	1200	8 oz	9600					
E806	L'Eau de Citron Cologne	42 1/2n	1020	8 oz	8160					
E805	L'Eau de Jasmin Cologne	42 1/2n	1020	8 oz	8160					
E807	L'Eau de Rose Cologne	70n	1680	8 oz	13440					
E801	L'Eau de Pomme Cologne	160	3840	8 oz	30720					
E802	L'Eau d'Abricot Cologne	97 1/2	2340	8 oz	18720					
E803	L'Eau de Teint Cologne	109	2616	8 oz	20928					
R320	Apple Oil	25n	600	6 oz	3600					
Q291	Magnolia Oil	221n	5304	8 oz	42432					
R315	Apple Oil	114	2736	4 oz	10944					
A608	Lemon Oil	104	2496	6 oz	14976					
A603	Lemon Oil	106n	2544	4 oz	10176					
A601	Lemon Oil	372	8928	2 oz	17856					
	Storeroom Total	4788 5/6	114932		735536					
SHIPPING DOCK:										
E806	L'Eau de Citron Cologne	20n	480	8 oz	3840					
E807	L'Eau de Rose Cologne	40n	960	8 oz	7680					
H84	Hand Creme	120	2880*	4 oz	11520					
Q291	Magnolia Oil	10n	240	8 oz	1920					
E801	L'Eau de Pomme Cologne	30n	720	8 oz	5760					
L818	Smoothing Lotion	80	1920*	8 oz	15360					
A603	Lemon Oil	40	960	4 oz	3840					
	Shipping Dock Total	340	8160		49920					
	Total Inventory	5128 5/6	123092		785456					
C	After testing 30 unopened cases, bottle count on vendor's label accepted on unopened cases.									
n	Test counted during observation. No errors observed.									
NOTE:	No obsolete or damaged inventory was observed.									
NOTE:	For cutoff last receiving report #12−05 was used on 12/30/02. 83 1/3 cases of #A601 Lemon Oil									
	were received from Fruit Scents, Inc. That shipment included in above inventory.									
	(On 1/24/03, I traced shoipment to voucher #12-29. JWP)									
*	On 1/24/03, traced into client's final priced inventory, working paper (C−1). JWP									

C-3
1-23-03
JWP

Apple Blossom Cologne Company
Inventory Observation Memo
December 31, 2002

I arrived at the client's plant at 1308 Bee Hive Boulevard, Chicago, Illinois, at 8:00 AM on January 1, 2003, to observe the client's physical inventory. The plant was closed this day for the inventory counting. I reviewed the client's inventory instructions, which appeared adequate. I then observed the client personnel as they took a 100% inventory. I recorded test counts for later tracing to the client's final priced inventory (C-2).

The client's housekeeping was good and the inventory neat and orderly to facilitate an accurate count. The client's plant is divided into two inventory areas: the main storeroom and the shipping dock. All inventory is received from vendors in 24-bottle cases.

In my opinion, the client used good inventory procedures and took an accurate count. The client's inventory personnel seemed competent and good control was exercised throughout the inventory procedures. Since the plant was shut down, inventory cutoff was not a problem. The last shipment of inventory was received on 12/30/02 from Fruit Scents Inc. (83 1/3 cases of #A601 Lemon Oil) and is included in the inventory count. I did not observe any obsolete or damaged inventory.

Jasper W. Parsons
Audit Senior
1-1-03

Apple Blossom Cologne Company — D-1

Prepaid Insurance and Insurance Expense — 1-23-03

12-31-02 — JWP

	Insurer	Policy Number	Type of Coverage	Amount of Coverage	Term of coverage From	Term of coverage To		Begin Balance 12-31-01	Premium Paid 2,002	Insurance Expense	Ending Balance 12-31-02
	Southwestern Fire	1628-41-8001 CE	Fire and extended	1,500,000	7-1-01	7-1-03		13171 N	-0-	8781 R	4390 R
	and Casualty		coverage – plant,								
			building, and contents.								
	Old Line Insurance	A2604282 C	Truck Liability	500,000	3-31-01	3-31-02		1054 N	-0-	1054 R	-0- R
	Group	A2604283 CE	Truck Liability	500,000	3-31-02	3-31-03		-0- N	4918 CY	3689 R	1229 R
	Illinois State Mutual	60-218049	Insurance on automobile								
			fleet:								
			Liability CE	50X-100X-10X	10-1-01	10-1-04		16228 N	-0-	5901 R	10327 R
			Collision CE	$100 DED.	10-1-01	10-1-04		11978 N	-0-	4356 R	7622 R
			Comprehensive CE	$100 DED.	10-1-01	10-1-04		6955 N	-0-	2529 R	4426 R
	American Fidelity and	XX6034 C	Fidelity bonds on	200,000	6-30-99	6-30-02		1152 N	-0-	1152 R	-0- R
	Casualty	XX8034 CE	employees	200,000	6-30-02	6-30-05		-0- N	8810 CY	1468 R	7342 R
								50538	13728	28930	35336
N	Agreed to prior year audit working papers.					Audit adjustments:				(TB-35)	(TB-BS)
E	Examined insurance policy noting coverage, term, and premium.					None				-0-	-0-
	All policies were in company safe.					Balance per audit				28930	35336
C	Details confirmed by insurance agency. Reference working paper (B-2).										
Y	Examined approved cash voucher and vendor invoice.										
R	Recalculated.										

Apple Blossom Cologne Company D-2
Insurance Confirmation 1-28-03
December 31, 2002 JWP

Pierce and Langdohl Insurance Agency

5806 Brunt Road
Chicago, Illinois 60616
Phone 312-555-3804

January 14, 2003

Anderson, Olds and Watershed
Certified Public Accountants
615 Big City Bank Building
Chicago, Illinois 60612

This is to confirm that during 2002, Apple Blossom Cologne Company had the following insurance policies listed with this agency:

Southwestern Fire and Casualty: Policy #4628-41-8001, fire and extended coverage on plant building and contents, $1,500,000, dated July 1, 2001, 2-year term, premium $17,562.

Old Line Insurance Group: Policy # AB6048R2, truck liability, $500,000, dated March 31, 2001, 1-year term, premium $4,215. Policy #AB6048R3, Truck liability, $500,000, dated March 31, 2002, 1-year term, premium $4,918.

State Mutual: Policy #60-218049, public liability (50K-100K-10K), collision ($100 ded.), and comprehensive ($100 ded.), dated October 1, 2001, 3-year term, premiums $17,703--liability, $13,067--collision, and $7,587--comprehensive.

American Fidelity and Casualty: Policy #KH-6034, fidelity bonds on employees, $200,000, dated June 30, 1999, 3-year term, premium $6,913. Policy #KH-8034, fidelity bond on employees, $250,000, dated June 30, 2002, 3-year term, premium $8,810.

Sincerely yours,

William J. Ruppersen, Agent
PIERCE AND LANGDOHL AGENCY

* Noted renewal of expired policy.

WIR/jap

I performed analytical procedures on the accounts, Prepaid Rent, Office Supplies Inventory, Small Tools Inventory, as well as the related expense accounts, to provide explanations for any fluctuations. The following results were obtained:

Account	Balance 12-31-01	Balance 12-31-02	Dollar Change	Percent Change
Prepaid rent	1250	5000	3750	300%
Rent expense	3750	3750	-0-	0%
Office supplies	5071	8657	3586	71%
Office supp. exp.	8211	9683	1472	18%
Small tools	3345	7162	3817	114%
Small tools exp.	2655	3359	704	27%

Although the percentage changes in many of these accounts are high, the dollar fluctuations are relatively small and not material. The changes are accounted for as follows:

Prepaid Rent

The Company leases a warehouse under a ten-year operating lease agreement executed on May 1, 2000. The terms of the agreement call for an advanced payment of $7,500 every two years beginning May 1, 2000. At that time the Company paid $7,500. The Company expensed 8 months in 2000 ($2,500), leaving 16 months or $5,000 remaining. After expensing 12 months ($3,750) of this balance in 2001, a balance of $1,250 remained. The Company made another $7,500 payment on May 1, 2002 and expensed $3,750 in 2002.

The asset balance will alternate between $5,000 in even numbered years and $1,250 in odd numbered years, while the expense will be $3,750 per year. Thus the asset account appears correctly stated at $5,000 (TB-BS) as does the expense at $3,750 (TB-IS). I examined the lease agreement in the permanent file.

<u>Office Supplies and Small Tools Inventory</u>

The dollar changes are not material; the client explained that the fluctuations reflect increases in sales and operating costs. In addition, I was present at January 1, 2003 to observe the taking of the office supplies and small tools inventories. The asset accounts for Office Supplies and Small Tools Inventory appear to be reasonably stated at $8,657 (TB-BS) and $7,162 (TB-BS) respectively.

The expense accounts also appear to be reasonably stated at $9,683 (TB-IS) and $3,359 (TB-IS), respectively.

Jasper W. Parsons
Audit Senior
January 28, 2003

Apple Blossom Cologne Company — E-1

Investments in Securities — 1-27-03

12-31-02 — JWP

Security	Balance 12-31-01	Additions	Disposals (sales)	Balance 12-31-02	Price per Share	Market Value	Holding Gain/Loss		
Southwestern Telecom	128250 J			128250 #	85 T	121125	(7125)		
Common @ $90	(1425 Sh)			(1425 Sh)					
United Grain	198948 J			198948 #	111 T	187146	(11802)		
Common @ $118	(1686 Sh)			(1686 Sh)					
Lackawanna Energy		C 147320	Y E*	147320 #	136 T	172720	25400		
Common @ $116		(1270 Sh)		(1270 Sh)					
Totals	327198	147320		474518		480991	6473		
				(TB-BS)		M			
					Client bal. 12/31/02		4496		
		Audit adjustments:				AJE #7	1977		
		Balance per audit		474518			6473		

J Traced to prior year's audit working papers.

E Examined broker's advice.

T Traced to share price quotation in Wall Street Journal, January 2, 2003

Y Traced to cash disbursements journal and supporting voucher.

\# Inspected security--Reference schedule (E-2).

C Confirmed by broker--Reference working paper (E-4).

* Cost properly includes brokers fee.

M Market exceeds cost. Propose (AJE #7) to record unrealized holding gain on securities.

Allowance for unrealized gain/loss on investments	116	1977	
Unrealized gain/loss on investments	506		1977

Analysis of allowance account:	
Balance per client at 12/31/02	4496
Required balance per analysis above	6473
Required adjustment	1977

Apple Blossom Cologne Company	E-2
Securities Examination	1-22-03
12-31-02	JWP

The following securities were examined at a safety deposit box at Big City National Bank registered in the name of Apple Blossom Cologne Co.

	Certificate Number		Number of Shares
Southwestern Telecom	21		1425
			(E-1)
Lackawanna Energy	8034		1270
			(E-1)
United Grain	6001		1686

The above listed securities were examined in my presence and returned to me intact on December 31, 2002 at 1:30 pm.

Lillian Stockton
Treasurer, Apple Blossom
Cologne Company

Apple Blossom Cologne Company — E-3

Gain/Loss on Sale of Investments — 1-27-03

12-31-02 — JWP

Date	Security	Number of Shares	Cost	Proceeds	Gain (Loss)
	None sold				

Apple Blossom Cologne Company — F-2

Additions to Property, Plant, and Equipment — 1-27-03

12-31-02 — JWP

(Prepared by Client)

Vo. No.	Vendor	Item Description	Cost	
3-26	Taggart Construction	Construction of garage	33013	AF@
	Chicago, FL	& maintenance shop for		
		automobile fleet.		
5-18	Bobbie Butler Ford	1999 GLC	9300	AF@
	Chicago, FL			
7-20	Hart-Murphy Office	Four (4) used IBM	4380	AF@
	Outfitters	computers for office		
	Chicago, FL	with one yr. service		
		contract @ $1095 ea.		
7-21	Hart-Murphy Office	Eight Kardex filing	2278	AF@
	Outfitters	cabinets at $284.75 ea.		
	Chicago, FL			
10-14	Edwards and Johnson	Atwell-Henley box	5045	AF@
	Industrial Supply Co.	folding machine		
	St. Louis, MO			
	Per client		54016	(1)
	Audit adjustments:		^ (F-1)	
	Per audit		54016	

SUMMARY ADDITIONS PER AUDIT ANALYSIS:

Voucher	Buildings	Machinery	Auto	Office	Total
3-26	33013 N				33013
5-18			9300 N		9300
7-20				4380 N	4380
7-21				2278 N	2278
10-14		5045 N			5045
Totals	33013	5045	9300	6658	54016
	^	^	^	^	
	(F-1)	(F-1)	(F-1)	(F-1)	(1)

N Agree with classification of each asset.

A Vouched to vendor's invoice.

^ Footed.

F Physically observed the asset.

@ Noted approval of addition in minutes of Board of Directors meeting.

Apple Blossom Cologne Company — F-3
Retirements of Property, Plant, and Equipment — 1-29-03
12-31-02 — JWP
(Prepared by Client)

Journal Vo. No.	Asset Description	Date Acquired	Date Sold	Depreciation Rate-Method	Cost	Accum. Deprec.	Book Value	Proceeds	Gain (Loss) on Disposal
3-12	Vacant lot located at	2-12-91 @	3-20-99 e	---	21000 @	-0- r	21000 r	39638 y	18638 r
	1212 Westminster Road				(F-1)	(F-1)			
	Chicago, Illinois								
		Per client			21000	-0-	21000	39638	18638
					^	^	^	^	^^
		Audit adjustments:							(TB-FS)
		Balance per audit			21000	-0-	21000	39638	18638

^ Footed.
^^ Crossfooted.
@ Agreed with fixed asset subsidiary ledger.
r Recalculated mathematical operation.
y Traced to cash receipts journal.
e Disposal of fixed asset authorized by Board of Directors per minutes.

Apple Blossom Cologne Company	F-4
Depreciation Computation	1-27-03
12-31-02	JWP
(Prepared by client)	

	Asset	Amount	Rate	2002 Deprec. Provision	Totals
	BUILDINGS:				
	Held full year #	243250	3.33%	8108 R	
	Additions @	33013	1.67%	550 R	
	Retirements &	-0-	1.67%		8658
	MACH. & EQUIPMENT:				(F-1)
	Held full year #	535800	5.00%	26790 R	
	Additions @	5045	2.50%	126 R	
	Retirements &	-0-	2.50%		26916
	AUTOMOTIVE :				(F-1)
	Held full year #	90125	25.00%	22531 R	
	Additions @	9300	12.50%	1162 R	
	Retirements &	-0-	12.50%		23693
	OFFICE FURN & FIXTURES:				(F-1)
	Held full year #	99775	5.00%	4989 R	
	Additions @	6658	2.50%	166 R	
	Retirements &	-0-	2.50%		5155
					(F-1)
	Per client			64422	64422
	Audit adjustments:			^	^
					(F-1)
	Per audit				64422
NOTE:	Assets held for full year computed by deducting retirements from beginning balance.	JWP			
NOTE:	One-half year's depreciation is recorded for all additions and retirements regardless of date of acquisition or disposal.	JWP			
NOTE:	Asset lives appear reasonable, as does depreciation expense.				
NOTE:	Depreciation rates agree with those used in prior year.				
^	Footed.				
R	Recomputed mathematical operation.				
#	Amounts traced to prior year's working papers.				
@	Amounts traced to working paper (F-2).				
&	Amounts traced to working paper (F-3).				

Apple Blossom Cologne Company — F-5

Repairs and Maintenance Account — 1-28-03

12-31-02 — JWP

(Prepared by client)

Vo. No.	Vendor	Item Description	Cost	
2-18	Smith and Louis Contractors	Repair leaks in the roof of warehouse.	895	u
3-4	Meyer Belt and Conveyor	Repair torn conveyor belt in boxing area.	518	u
5-40	Lone Wolf Painting	Repaint plant offices.	6400	u
10-16	Alex McBane Heat. & Air Cond.	Annual servicing of furnace & heating systems	2686	u
11-28	Texas Metals	Repair and replace handrails on shipping dock.	3358	u
			13857	
		Vouchers less than $500 not listed.	4012	
		Per client	17869	
		Audit adjustments:	^	
			(TB-TS)	
		Balance per audit	17869	

^ Footed

u Examined vouchers and supporting documents. Reasonably classified as repairs and maintenance.

Apple Blossom Cologne Company			G–1
Accounts Payable			1–28–03
12–31–02			JWP
(Prepared by client)			

Vo. No.	Vendor	Amount	
11–18	Fruit Scents, Inc.	89880	uyC (G–3)
12–15	Edwards, Overstreet & Gilley	3600	uy
12–28	Flash Freight Co.	4461	uy
12–29	Fruit Scents, Inc.	14000	uyC (G–3)
12–32	Fruit Juicy Perfume Co.	85875	uyC (G–4)
12–34	Steck Hamilton	2300	uy
12–36	Hammel, Hammel & Johnson	6725	uy
12–37	Fruit Scents, Inc.	14295	uyC (G–3)
	Per client 12–31–02	221136	
		^	
	Audit adjustments:	(TB–BS)	
	(AJE #5) (G–2)	2025	
	Balance per audit	223161	

^ Footed

u Traced to cash disbursements journal. Paid after 1–1–03.

y Vouched to vendor's invoice and other supporting documents. All items received on or before year-end, 12–31–02.

C Confirmed.

Peach Blossom Cologne Company — G-2

Search for Unrecorded Liabilities — 1-27-03

12-31-02 — JWP

Vo. No.	Vendor	Invoice Date/ Terms		Comments		Un-recorded Amount	
1-14	Central Power & Light	12-27-02		December services		2025	X
						2025	

X Vouched to vendor's invoice and other supporting documents. Represents December service or merchandise. Propose (AJE #5):

		Dr.	Cr.
830	Utilities expense	2025	
301	Accounts payable		2025

NOTE: Reviewed all cash vouchers and supporting documents for period January 1, 2003 to January 10, 2003, as well as unmatched invoice and receiver files for period January 1, 2003 to January 24, 2003. No January vouchers represented merchandise or services on or prior to December 31, 2002, except as noted.

Apple Blossom Cologne Company
Attorney's Letter
December 31, 2002

A.L./G-5
1 of 2
2-4-03
JWP

Edwards, Overstreet, and Gilley

Attorneys at Law

1604 South Fourth . Chicago, Illinois 60614
Phone: 312-555-3892
Fax: 312-555-9998

January 21, 2003

Anderson, Olds and Watershed
Certified Public Accountants
615 Big City National Bank Building
Main at Michigan Avenue
Chicago, Illinois 60612

Re: Apple Blossom Cologne Company

Dear Sir or Madam:

By letter dated January 3, 2003, Mr. Lawrence Lancaster of Apple Blossom Cologne Company (The "Company") has requested us to furnish you with certain information in connection with your examination of the accounts of the Company as of December 31, 2002. While this firm represents the Company on a regular basis, our engagement has been limited to specific matters as to which we were consulted by the Company.

Subject to the foregoing and to the last paragraph of this letter we advise you that since January 1, 2002 we have not been engaged to give substantive attention to, or represent the Company in connection with material loss contingencies coming within the scope of clause (a) of Paragraph 5 of the Statement of Policy referred to in the last paragraph of this letter.

The information set forth herein is as of the date of this letter and we disclaim any undertaking to advise you of changes which thereafter may be brought to our attention.

This response is limited by, and in accordance with, the ABA Statement of Policy Regarding Lawyers' Responses to Auditors' Requests for Information (December 1975); without limiting the generality of the foregoing, the limitation set forth in such Statement on the scope and use of this response (Paragraphs 2 and 7) are specifically incorporated herein by reference, and any description herein of any "loss contingencies" is qualified in its entirety by Paragraph 5 of the Statement and the accompanying Commentary (which is an integral part of the Statement).

(Continued)

Page Two

Consistent with the last sentence of Paragraph 6 of the ABA Statement of Policy and pursuant to the Company's request, this will confirm as correct the Company's understanding as set forth in its audit inquiry letter to us that whenever, in the course of performing legal services for the Company with respect to a matter recognized to involve an unasserted possible claim or assessment that may call for financial statement disclosure, we have formed a professional conclusion that the Company must disclose or consider disclosure concerning such possible claim or assessment, we, as a matter of professional responsibility to the Company, will so advise the Company and will consult with the Company concerning the question of such disclosure and the applicable requirements of Statement of Financial Accounting Standards No. 5.

Very truly yours,

EDWARDS, OVERSTREET AND GILLEY

Michael Overstreet

Michael Overstreet
Partner

Apple Blossom Cologne Company

1308 Beehive Boulevard Chicago, Illinois 60615
Phone: 312-477-7288
Fax: 312-477-9999
Internet: www.appleblossom.com

February 5, 2003

Anderson, Olds and Watershed
Certified Public Accountants
615 Big City National Bank Building
Main at Michigan
Chicago, Illinois 60612

The following representations are made to you in connection with your examination of the financial statements of Apple Blossom Cologne Company as of December 31, 2000 for the purpose of expressing an opinion as to whether the financial statements present fairly, in all material respects, the financial position, results of operations, and cash flows of Apple Blossom Cologne Company in conformity with generally accepted accounting principles.

We confirm that we are responsible for the statement of financial position, results of operations, and cash flows in conformity with generally accepted accounting principles. Certain representations in this letter are described as being limited to matters that are material. Items are considered material, regardless of size, if they involve an omission or misstatement of accounting information that, in the light of surrounding circumstances, makes it probable that the judgment of a reasonable person relying on the information would be changed or influenced by the omission or misstatement.

We further confirm that the following representations made to you during your audit examination are accurate to the best of our knowledge and belief:

Financial Statements
The financial statements referred to above are fairly presented in conformity with generally accepted accounting principles. All material transactions have been properly recorded in the accounting records underlying the financial statements. No fraud exists involving management or employees who have significant roles in internal control or others that could have a material effect on the financial statements. No shortages or irregularities have been discovered that have not been disclosed to you, and to our knowledge there is nothing reflecting upon the honesty of members of our organization. The company has no plans that could materially affect the carrying value or classification of assets or liabilities.

 Continued

Receivables
Trade Accounts receivable in the amount of $__139,504__ are valid receivables and do not include any amounts for goods shipped on consignment or approval. In our opinion, the balance in Allowance for Bad Debts of
$__11,889__ is sufficient to cover any losses, discounts, or allowances that may be incurred or allowed in the collection of the receivables.

Inventories:
The Company's inventory in the amount of $__873,766__ as determined by actual count by competent employees under the supervision of management as of December 31, 2002 are fairly stated on the first-in, first-out, lower-of-cost-or-market basis. Reasonable allowance has been made for slow-moving, obsolete, unsaleable, or unusable items. All inventories are the property of the Company. Inventory balances do not include (1) amounts of goods consigned to the Company, (2) merchandise billed to customers on or before the inventory date, or (3) any items for which the liability has not been provided on the books.

Property, Plant, and Equipment:
Property, plant and equipment is owned with satisfactory title. Capitalizable charges and purchased additions during the year are stated at cost. Property disposed of or abandoned was removed from the accounts. The provision for depreciation in the amount of $__64,422__ was determined on a basis consistent with preceding years. In our opinion, depreciation methods used and depreciable lives assigned are appropriate for allocating the cost of the assets over their useful lives. The valuation account, accumulated depreciation (balance of $316,661), is reasonably adequate to state property, plant, and equipment assets at a reasonable book value with respect to the utilization expected over their remaining lives.

Owned Assets:
The Company had satisfactory title to all owned assets at December 31, 2002. All significant mortgages, assignments, pledges, or other encumbrances of assets have been disclosed to you.

Liabilities:
With the possible exception of a few minor amounts, all direct liabilities of the Company amount to $__649,331__ and were recorded on the books as of December 31, 2002.

There are no:

a. Violations or possible violations of laws or regulations whose effects should be considered for disclosure in the financial statements or as a basis for recording a loss contingency.
b. Unasserted claims or assessments that our lawyer has advised us are probable of assertion and must be disclosed in accordance with FASB Statement No. 5, Accounting for Contingencies.

Continued

c. Other liabilities or gain or loss contingencies that are required to be accrued or disclosed by FASB Statement No. 5.

The Company had no other contingent or possible liabilities that have not been disclosed to you.

Purchase and Sales Commitments:
At December 31, 2002, the Company had no important unfilled contracts for purchases in excess of normal requirements or at prices substantially in excess of market, or for sales at prices that are expected to result in a loss.

Capital Stock:
All capital stock issued or reserved for options, warrants, or other future issuance is disclosed in the financial statements.

Minutes:
We have made available to you (1) all financial records and related data, and (2) minutes of the meetings of stockholders, directors, and committees of directors, or summaries of actions of recent meetings for which minutes have not yet been prepared. Minutes of such meetings as exhibited to you are complete and authentic records of all such meetings held during the period from January 1, 2002 through December 31, 2002.

General:
No events have occurred and no facts have been discovered since December 31, 2002, which would make the balance sheet at that date or the statement of earnings for the year then ended materially inaccurate or misleading.

No charges are pending against the Company for alleged violations of federal, state, or local laws, which would have any material effect on the financial statements. No communications from regulatory agencies have been received concerning noncompliance with or deficiencies in financial reporting practices.

The company has complied with all aspects of contractual agreements that would have a material effect on the financial statements in the event of noncompliance.

No director, officer, or principal holder of the Company's equity securities was indebted (except for minor amounts for ordinary travel and expenses) to the Company at any time during the year.

The following have been properly recorded or disclosed in the financial statements:

a. Related-party transactions, including sales, purchases, loans, transfers, leasing arrangements,

Continued

Page Four

and guarantees, and amounts receivable from or payable to related parties.

b. Guarantees, whether written or oral, under which the company is contingently liable.

c. Significant estimates and material concentrations known to management that are required to be disclosed in accordance with the AICPA□s Statement of Position 94-6 (Disclosure of Certain Significant Risks and Uncertainties). (Significant estimates are estimates at the balance sheet date that could change materially within the next year; concentrations refer to volumes of business, revenues, available sources of supply, or markets or geographic areas for which events could occur that would significantly disrupt normal finances within the next year.)

Very truly yours,

Lawrence Lancaster
President
Apple Blossom Cologne Company

Parker Shelton
Controller
Apple Blossom Cologne Company

Apple Blossom Cologne Company — G-7
Contingent Liabilities and Subsequent Events — 2-5-03
December 31, 2002 — JWP

Inquiry was made of Mr. Lancaster, President, Mr. Shelton, Controller, and Ms. Stockton, Treasurer, concerning possible contingent liabilities and events occurring subsequent to the balance sheet date that may require accrual or disclosure in the financial statement.

The client's legal counsel, Edwards, Overstreet, and Gilley reported in their letter to us (Schedule (A.L./G-5)) that they knew of no direct or contingent liabilities arising from past or present litigation.

I also examined the minutes of the meetings of the Board of Directors and the client's contract files, inquired of management, and reviewed subsequent year□s journals and ledgers, searching for possible contingent liabilities and subsequent events. Nothing was found to indicate the existence of any contingent liabilities or subsequent events.

On the basis of my examination, it is my opinion that no contingent liabilities exist at 12-31-02 and that no subsequent events have occurred requiring accrual or disclosure.

Jasper W. Parsons
Audit Senior
February, 5, 2003

Peach Blossom Cologne Company
Unrecorded Liability Search
December 31, 2002

G-8
2-5-03
JWP

I reviewed all cash vouchers and supporting documents for the period 1-1-03 to 1-10-03, as well as unmatched invoice and receiver files for the period 1-1-03 to 1-24-03. No January vouchers represented merchandise or services prior to January 1, 2003, except as noted on W/P (G-2).

A review of transactions within the interest and professional fees operating accounts, as well as a review of the minutes of the Board of Directors' meetings, indicated that there were no unrecorded note obligations or litigation contingencies.

Confirmation from client's legal counsel indicated that no pending litigation, direct, or contingent liabilities exist for the Company. Reference attorney's letter (A.L./G-5).

A letter of representations was obtained. Regarding liabilities, that letter indicated that all direct liabilities of the company were recorded and all contingent liabilities had been disclosed to our auditing firm. The letter revealed no apparent unrecorded liabilities. The letter of representations is referenced (L.O.R./G-6).

Standard bank confirmations were obtained. The Big City National Bank confirmation identified a note payable to that bank. This note was recorded by the client as indicated on W/P (I-1).

Excerpts from minutes of the Board of Directors' meetings are included in the permanent file materials. The minutes revealed no items resulting in unrecorded liabilities.

Accordingly, no unrecorded liabilities were found.

Jasper W. Parsons
Audit Senior
February 5, 2003

Apple Blossom Cologne Company	H-1
Accrued Payroll Taxes	1-27-03
12-31-02	JWP
(Prepared by client)	

	Balance 12-31-01		Additions		Pay-ments		Balance 12-31-02
F.I.C.A. Tax	39,948	γ	169,716	*	178,807	t	30,857
Medicare	10,529	γ	41,286	*	44,308	t	7,507
State Unemployment	-0-	γ	9,576	*	9,576	t	-0-
Federal Unemployment	-0-	γ	2,016	*	2,016	t	-0-
Withholding Tax	54,459	γ	213,551	*	229,183	t	38,827
Balance per client	104,936		436,145		463,890		77,191
	^		^		^		^^
Audit adjustments:							(TB-BS)
(AJE #6) (H-2)							36,655
Balance per audit							113,846

*Payroll Tax Computation	F.I.C.A.		Medicare	State Unemp	Fed. Unemp
Total wages 2002 per client	1,423,672	B	1,423,672	1,423,672	1,423,672
Less Wages over FICA Max. $76,200	55,000				
Less Wages over Unemp. Max. $7,000				1,171,672	1,171,672
Wages Taxed	1,368,672		1,423,672	252,000	252,000
X Tax Rate	6.2%		1.45%	3.8%	0.8%
Employer Expense	84,858		20,643	9,576	2,016
Employee	84,858		20,643		
Totals per client	169,716		41,286	9,576	2,016

Total wage expense:	
Expense per client	1,423,672
	(TB-IS)
(AJE #6) (H-2)	105,028
Balance per audit	1,528,700

Total employer payroll tax expense:	
FICA	84,858
Medicare	20,643
State Unemployment	9,576
Federal Unemployment	2,016
Payroll tax per client	117,093
Audit adjustments	(TB-IS)
(AJE #6) (H-2)	12,866
Balance per audit	129,959

^ Footed

^^ Footed and crossfooted

γ Agreed to prior years working papers.

* Agrees to total withheld per payroll records.

t Traced to cash disbursements journal, examined paid vouchers and vouched amounts to employer copies of quarterly 941 forms, form 940, and state unemployment tax return.

B Traced to trial balance

Apple Blossom Cologne Company — H-2

Wages and Salaries Payable — 1-29-03

12-31-02 — JWP

	No. of Emplees	Gross	Withold. Tax (15%)	FICA (6.2%)	Medicare (1.45%)	Net	FICA (6.2%)	Medicare (1.45%)	SUTA (3.8%)	FUTA (0.8%)	Total
Hourly (Paid weekly.)	14	7,538 y	1,131 c	467 c	109 c	5,831	467 c	109 c	286 c	60 c	922
week ended 12-27-02											
(to be paid 1-3-03)											
Stub period 12-30 &	14	3,015 y	452 c	187 c	44 c	2,332	187 c	44 c	115 c	24 c	370
12-31-02 (to be						8,163 d					
paid 1-10-03)											
Salaried (Paid monthly)											
Administration	3	14,758 ye	2,214 c	915 c	214 c	11,415	915 c	214 c	561 c	118 c	1,808
Plant Operation	7	28,908 ye	4,336 c	1,792 c	419 c	22,361	1,792 c	419 c	1,099 c	231 c	3,541
Sales	7	30,250 ye	4,538 c	1,876 c	439 c	23,397	1,876 c	439 c	1,150 c	242 c	3,707
Controller	3	11,842 ye	1,776 c	734 c	172 c	9,160	734 c	172 c	450 c	95 c	1,451
Treasurer	2	8,717 ye	1,308 c	540 c	126 c	6,743	540 c	126 c	331 c	70 c	1,067
						73,076 d					
Totals		105,028	15,755	6,511	1,523	81,239	6,511	1,523	3,992	840	12,866
						(TB-BS adjusted)					

Propose (AJE # 6) to record accrued payroll:

Wage and salary expense	820	105028	
Payroll tax expense	821	12866	
Accrued payroll taxes	302		36655
Wages and salaries payable	303		81239

c Calculated

y Traced wage and salary rates to payroll register

d Traced to cash disbursements journal noting payment after 12-31-02.

e Agreed to Board of Directors' minutes.

Apple Blossom Cologne Company H-3
Analytical Procedures Performed on Accrued Liabilities 1-29-03
December 31, 2002 JWP

I performed analytical procedures on the accounts, Dividends Payable and Accrued Property Taxes, to provide explanations for any fluctuations. The following results were obtained:

Account	Balance 12-31-01	Balance 12-31-02	Dollar Change	Percent Change
Dividends payable	13875	17575	3700	27%
Accrued prop. tax	9500	14113	4613	49%

Although the percentage changes in these accounts are high, the fluctuations are explained as follows:

Dividends Payable

The balance of $17,575 agrees with the Board of Directors' meeting of December 6, 2002 per excerpts from the minutes of that meeting filed in the permanent file working papers. Dividend of $1.90 per share was declared payable on January 17, 2003 to shareholders of record at December 31, 2002 with 9250 shares outstanding ($1.90 x 9250 = $17,575). The increase in the account is explained by the increase in the dividend from $1.50 per share in 2001 to $1.90 per share in 2002. I traced the dividend payment to the cash disbursements journal in January 2003. The account appears to be reasonably stated at $17,575.
(TB-BS)

Accrued Property Taxes

Property taxes for any year are assessed on the beginning balance of inventory plus the depreciated value of fixed assets, which amounted to $1,279,961 in 2001 and $1,408,100 in 2002. Tax expense decreased from $14,793 in 2001 to $14,113 in 2002 as a result of a decrease in the effective tax rate from 2001 to 2002. In 2001, the effective tax rate was .011557. In 2002, the effective rate had decreased to .010023, calculated as follows:

	Assessed Value Percentage		Rate		
City	.75	x	.0107(1)	=	.008025
County	.27	x	.0074(2)	=	.001998
			Effective tax rate		.010023

(1)$1.07 per $100 of assessed value.
(2)$0.74 per $100 of assessed value.

2002 tax expense: .010023 x $1,408,100 = $14,113
(TB-BS)

I traced the payments made in January 2002 and January 2003 to the cash disbursements journal; the 49% increase in the accrual results from the client having paid $5,293 of the $14,793 property tax prior to the end of 2001 and the $9.500 balance in January 2002. The Accrued Property Tax account appears to be reasonably stated at $14,113 at December 31, 2002.
(TB-BS)

Jasper W. Parsons
Audit Senior

	Apple Blossom Cologne Company				H-4	
	Federal Income Taxes Payable				2-3-03	
	12-31-02				JWP	
	(Prepared by client)					
					Tax Liability	Tax Expense
	Balance 12-31-02				14230	
	Additions: 2002 taxes				80000	80000
	Payments:				94230	
	Final payment Jan. 2002					
	on 2001 taxes			14230		
	First quarter deposit, 2002 taxes			20000		
	Second quarter deposit, 2002 taxes			20000		
	Third quarter deposit, 2002 taxes			20000	74230	
	Balance 12-31-02, per client				20000	80000
					^	^
(1)	Adjustments to income tax and income tax				(TB-BS)	(TB-IS)
	liability resulting from audit adjustments.					
	Reference (AJE # 8) to record tax adjustment:					
		940 Federal income tax expense				43772
			307 Federal income taxes payable		43772	
	Balance per audit				63772	123772
	(1) INCOME TAX EXPENSE PER AUDIT:					
	15%	50000			7500	
	25%	25000			6250	
	34%	75000	$323,595		110022	
		Per audit			123772	
		Per client			80000	
	Required adjustment				43772	
^	Footed.					
@	Agreed to prior year's audit working papers.					
Y	Traced to cash disbursements journal.					

Apple Blossom Cologne Company
Memorandum Regarding Capital Stock Transactions
December 31, 2002

J-1
1-30-03
JWP

I examined the corporate minutes, the stock certificate subsidiary ledger, as well as the cash receipts and cash disbursements journals. They revealed no capital stock transactions during 2002. The balance in the Capital Stock and OtherContributed Capital accounts represent 9,250 shares issued and outstanding out of a total of 20,000 shares authorized. The balances in these accounts of \$925,000 (TB-BS) and \$736,550 (TB-BS), respectively appear to be reasonably stated at December 31, 2002.

Jasper W. Parsons
Audit Senior
January 29, 2003

Apple Blossom Cologne Company — K-1

Retained Earnings — 2-5-03

12-31-02 — JWP

	Balance 12-31-01	272435	A
		(TB-BS)	
	Dividends	17575	M
		(TB-BS)	
		254860	
	Net Income, 2002, before audit adjustments	441319	*
		(TB-BS)	
	Balance, 12-31-02, per client	696179	R
	Net effect of 2002 audit adjustments:		
	(Adjusting entries debit income $208,222)	(166496)	*
	Balance, 12-31-02, after audit adjustments	529683	C

* Agreed to income statement--working trial balance (TB-IS).

A Agreed to prior year's audit working papers.

M Traced to corporate minutes and to liability – Dividends payable.

R Reconciles to (TB-BS) per client.

C Reconciles to (TB-BS) per audit.